Spanish Style

Kate Hill
Photography by Tim Clinch

Spanish Style

MERRELL
LONDON · NEW YORK

Introduction

How does one define Spanish style? When photographer and English *bon vivant* Tim Clinch challenged me to a road trip to answer that very question, I wondered where we would even begin. Tim had lived in Madrid, Cadíz and the Andalucían countryside; I live in south-west France. Perhaps we'd meet on that historic scrawl of a road that threads through the 800 kilometres (500 miles) from the Pyrenees to Galicia in western Spain and ends in Baroque grandeur in front of Santiago de Compostela's sixteenth-century parador; or travel directly to the very south of Spain – Andalucía – where on a quiet hillside a private home basks in the Mediterranean sun while sea air blows through precisely furnished and lavish rooms. Eventually, we would meander to Catalunya to find a world-renowned restaurant on the site of which spectacular glass sleeping-houses have sprung from the local volcanic soil, and a solitary fisherman's *cabaña*, a retreat that epitomizes simplicity itself, anchored in a sea of olive-trees on Cap Creus. We chased the weather and the landscapes that led us from one distinct region to the next, and recorded this collection of exemplary homes and hotels, the places where Spaniards and international tourists alike delight in the exuberance that defines Spain and its design.

The attempt to identify Spanish style began with the land itself, this collection of varied regional idioms and cultures reflecting a vast peninsula surrounded by rugged coastlines, crowned by a mountain range, the Pyrenees, and harbouring a huge, open interior of weathered landscapes and fertile fields. As the album of

evocative photographs began to give shape to the place names that ring romantically across the Iberian peninsula — Galicia, Catalunya and Andalucía — I still searched for the mysterious ingredient that unites this diverse anthology of contemporary homes, world-renowned architecture and traditional hacienda estates.

At first, Spanish style seems a conundrum of contrasts. It is not new; yet it is totally contemporary. It is built on the solid structure and decorative use of noble materials, such as stone, wood, marble, tile and iron, and yet embraces the ephemeral movement of water and wind, light and shade. As familiar as a movie-set hacienda and as shocking as the elegant use of glass boxes for a four-star hotel, design is not only wrought in such elements as Baroque stone façades and tendrils of supple ironwork, but also defined by such empty spaces as the courtyards and plazas of every small village and large city. Surprises lie behind closed doors and cloistered beneath arcades, where we discover a savvy sort of insouciance based on comfort and fashion and above all celebrated in a distinctively Spanish lifestyle.

From the Basque Country in the north to southern Andalucía and across the width of the country from Galicia to Catalunya, we found a consistent attention to texture and detail, built on a respect for native materials and quality craftsmanship. The solid granite structure of Santiago de Compostela's classic parador shows its sixteenth-century bones as proudly as a traditional rush-and-stone vaulted ceiling in a Catalan *masia*, or farmhouse. From structure follows design, and the decorative aspects have evolved from these firm foundations of lasting, time-proven materials. In this sense Spanish style resembles a hall of mirrors in which one can look 'through' the past to see today's crystalline reflection in the mix of elements old and new.

The pace of life in Spain, as much as anything else, dictates its style; fast and industrious sprints of crafted design work are followed by the use of brilliant breaks of space that are as calm and restorative as the iconic afternoon siesta. Private and public spaces, such as courtyards and patios, weave together in a way that is born of mixed social interaction, as indicated by the range of young and old mingling, for example, during the evening *pasaje*, or ritual promenade, through city parks, in the streets and on beach fronts.

Modern Spain claims something from every antique culture that has touched its beaches or wilder shores, from the Phoenicians, Greeks and Romans to the Moors and northern Europeans; the Moorish walled cities of the south form a particularly eloquent testimony. History is evident in these architectural bones, the skeletal foundations laid down by stone-cutters and carpenters, which current designers respect. Structural materials are exposed and celebrated in ancient and modern terms, as Catalan vaulting, colonnaded arcades and *viga* (roof) rafters join woven titanium, pre-cast cement and glass walls in defining Spanish style. So what does this bring to the mix of rural and urban life now, at the beginning of a new century?

These photographs of homes, showcases, studios and destination hotels (the new weekend home, if you will) reveal the work of a group of designers who reflect

the past and its traditional craftsmanship and use of local materials while embracing the new style of international living that nourishes a dynamic contemporary society. Spanish style is a wide umbrella under which to gather an archive of twenty-first-century ideas of design united by attention to the exterior living-spaces as much as to the interiors.

Walls open out on to nature and seamlessly let a bare landscape drift into a pristine white room; an olive-grove surrounds an artist's studio that floats like a landlocked boat in the Mediterranean winds that blow the trees until they seem like a swirling silver sea; traditional wooden shutters keep the southern Andalucían sun at bay and woven mats hang like flags, throwing rooms into precious cool shadow. Courtyards and fountains invite casual gatherings, and colonnaded arcades shelter exterior rooms and art-filled corridors. A satellite image of Madrid's residential areas shows the prominence of these shaded courtyards surrounded by square roof lines.

Where the similarities end, the diversity of Spain's sense of design begins, embracing international design stars as well as celebrating traditional colour and texture. Even the most contemporary buildings connect old with new – epitomized in the way in which Frank Gehry's City of Wine for the Marqués de Riscal in Rioja links his avant-garde titanium-and-stainless-steel roof to the bare rootstock of local sandstone, matching the golden façade of the Baroque village church.

Colour is celebrated across the land on a foundation of stark and startling white stucco, from the blue-trimmed fishermen's cottages of Cadaqués to the walls of a grand Moorish hacienda in Seville. Black and white balance strong interior colours and form the background to a palette used with absolute confidence, as in the ceiling of purple and green rafters in a designer's home in Cadíz, or the red-on-red tones of a wine spa in Rioja. In these widely diverse interiors, colour is strong, definitive and vibrantly Spanish.

In the words of the Spanish architect Monica Rivera, 'The typical Spanish iconography, mostly related to the southern regions of Spain, is so strong that it sometimes overrides other conditions that are very different.' Rivera hopes that such preconceptions about Spain can be reconsidered; in her view, the country should be understood instead 'as an aggregation of complementary landscapes and cultures'.

We trust that these selected visions of a current and modern Spain that we discovered behind doors both private and public will help to broaden the notion of what that 'aggregation' includes, and the way in which it is rooted in a past that is a definitive part of the present and future of Spanish style.

Historic Hacienda
Ranch hotel, Andalucía

Across rolling fields of wheat and rice, the Cortijo El Esparragal sits in a time-warp world of dancing fountains, centenarian trees and horse-drawn carriages. The heavily varnished, iron-studded blue doors swing open to reveal the domestic life of a working ranch, or *cortijo*, as glimpsed in every corner of this gently restored hacienda. Founded in the seventeenth century as a monastery, the estate became a bull-raising ranch in the nineteenth century, and is now a 3000-hectare (7400-acre) cattle farm and guest house. A sense of the hacienda's history resonates in its quiet corners and shady courts: the visitor is at once guest of the present and voyeur of the past.

As one turns a tiled corner and enters a green courtyard, a flutter of guitar chords seems to sing out; but it is only a gentle rain, making a mockery of the central fountain. The scent of Seville oranges perfumes the surrounding bedrooms, and the rustle of palm fronds and branches plays on the spring air. El Esparragal lives in its past. Indian chintz, highly valued by early explorers, covers sofas and chairs that are placed cosily close to fireplaces and reading lamps. A tasselled cord opens a door, while the sleepy air of this historic hacienda exhales through shuttered windows.

Cortijo El Esparragal, surrounded by carefully groomed gardens, has monastic origins, evident in its cloistered entrance and chapel-bell façade.

Hacienda life, defined by the outside as much as the inside, revolves around a series of courtyards filled with flowering plants and hanging baskets. As in many hot countries, such courtyards act as extended living-spaces and places to receive visitors on gentle summer nights, as well as sheltering indoor living-spaces from winter weather. Birds serenade from hidden nests, and flowers perfume private corners; colourful old ceramics hang in covered walkways; a shaded spot set with tables and chairs offers a hint of bygone hospitality. The varied courtyards are a play of shadow and light, their columned arcades housing collections of local pottery and souvenirs of early ranch life. True to their original use, these courtyards punctuate buildings, creating small pockets of space, which once defined life here. Families were raised, meals were taken and love was declared amid the hidden corners of the rambling ranch house.

Although the courtyards and arcades are used in the hot summer months, during winter, plump English furniture breaks the large rooms into cosy areas for gatherings beside the fire. A large, wide salon easily welcomes a big crowd for winter suppers, under the watchful gaze of a painted cast of toreadors and flamenco dancers from the last two centuries, reminders of the Andalucían customs that are still enacted at weekends and on feast days. Similarly, scattered under arcades and throughout the hacienda, a vast gallery of paintings tells the history of Seville's corrida and accompanying fetes, of prized bulls, and of horses

LEFT, TOP AND BOTTOM Towering above the vast Andalucían plain, El Esparragal conceals a warren of private courtyards featuring melodic fountains that cool shaded patios.

at work demonstrating *doma vaquera* – a style of horse-riding used, along with a long staff called *la garrocha*, to work cattle.

From courtyard to salon to bedroom suites, the interior of El Esparragal conveys a gentlewomanly approach to ranch life. The traditionally masculine work of ranching and riding is left outside, while inside, the rooms are tempered by classic boudoir femininity, exemplified by red chintz curtains and an elegant writing-desk, or delicate Meissen figures that dance on mahogany side-tables beside red plaster carvings topping a book-filled niche. It is here, in these very personal and private corners of El Esparragal, that the long family history of ranchers and bull-breeders comes alive. Booted footsteps ring off polished tiles and on the stair risers, where a panorama of peasant life is depicted in coloured ceramics. The first floor harbours private salons and dining-rooms and a glassed-in balcony overlooking a shady terrace. Resembling a chapel as much as a gallery, the connecting hall features antique religious statues and paintings that once kept an eye on the comings and goings of centuries of monks and now observe a parade of international visitors.

But it is the massive and sprawling structure itself, separating as it does the pleasurable aspects of country life from the grind of a working ranch, that commands respect today. Immaculately painted and trimmed with both colourful and black borders that mimic the ubiquitous ironwork – hammered, forged and riveted – Cortijo El Esparragal proudly displays its heritage in the decorative particulars of classic rural architecture and iconographic Spanish details.

LEFT, TOP AND BOTTOM An icon-filled wide gallery leads through an immense carved door towards the staircase that descends to the chapel and private rooms.

OPPOSITE The capacious salon recalls the ranch's bull-breeding history, kept alive through sculpted mementoes of famous bullfighters and their bulls.

Style and Vision
Apartment, Madrid

The Madrid *pied-à-terre* of interior designer Gaspar Sobrino is a
delightful study in deception. The minuscule apartment of just 50 square
metres (540 sq. feet), neatly laid out in two main rooms, is decorated
with a larger vision, an inviting and contemporary take on urban living
that fits comfortably against a sunlit interior courtyard in the classic
residential building.

The tightly conceived space functions as both home and office, and
in its style is typical of Sobrino's work – a fresh look at old textures
presented in a new framework of modern materials. As if placing a bright
contemporary painting in a well-loved frame, Sobrino takes the edge
off the edgy and balances the everyday with the exceptional: the result,
at once familiar and fresh, evokes a simple emotional reaction.

The high-ceilinged sitting-room doubles as a design office for Sobrino
and his partner, who together, as Les Charmelites, specialize in window-
dressing and commercial interior design. When asked what his dream
project would be, Sobrino barely hesitates before saying, 'A hotel!'

'Money is not the most important thing in design', Sobrino continues.
'It's creativity. I don't like all-new design but seek something with soul.'
He calls this 'emotional intelligence' and talks about his way of working.
'I have some Arab blood. It's that Arabic feeling I have for a space, when
I enter, that is based on materials. Like a cool tile floor that was meant
to be walked on barefoot because shoes were shed on entering.'

A monochromatic palette of black, grey and white
provides the backdrop to Sobrino's design studio,
which doubles as his apartment. His signature bulldog –
immortalized here in the form of a bronze table lamp
and in a painting in the adjacent room – features in
many of his designs. A photographic portrait of Sobrino
hangs high above the fireplace.

This attention to surface and the emotive possibilities of tactile experience is evident on arriving, through a labyrinth of whitewashed halls. The hardwood entrance gives way to a charcoal-coloured sisal carpet that covers an 'uninteresting floor' and serves to counterpoise the lofty ceilings. 'I use neutral for the box, the frame, and then add strong colours. Strong, not strident, colours', Sobrino explains. The neutral theme continues as pearl-grey on all the walls, against which he has hung a very personal collection of colourful works by young artists, as well as some of his own designs. Strong – and definitely not strident – magenta, violet and saffron punctuate the sobriety with a joyful elegance.

Throughout the apartment, sumptuously weighted, embroidered fabrics, thrown across a sofa or covering a table, take on a sort of structural or sculptural form of their own. Woven textures, bright colours

ABOVE, LEFT A nineteenth-century marble bust of Queen Maria-Christina is a bright-white note against the neutral grey background used throughout the apartment.

ABOVE, RIGHT Sobrino's bronze canine muse offers creative inspiration at the office table that serves as the designer's studio.

OPPOSITE Glowing jewel-tone silks and woven textiles adorn the bed, which sits in a simple alcove. One of Sobrino's antlered mannequins watches over the scene.

and design harmonize with a black-and-white base, which includes the sofa and a large graphic diptych of Sobrino's signature icon, a bulldog. These bold gestures are offset by gentler ones: for example, a simple hemp flour-sack, a favourite souvenir from India, is framed in a place of honour above a classic white-marble fireplace.

'I like to feel each room and use materials that act out the room; a bedroom is meant for dreams, a bathroom must be warm – a place for our naked skin to be comfortable', Sobrino says.

In a tidy, square bedroom, custom-made for exotic dreams, the bed is laid with a silk sari as luxurious in colour as it is in texture, the jewel hues sparking brightly against the matt grey walls. An antlered mannequin character from a Sobrino window-dressing presides like an animistic guardian angel. Personal effects are displayed on industrial shelving or concealed in built-in corner storage, an economical solution to the quotidian needs of urban living.

This charming jewel-box two-room apartment in the heart of Madrid's chic Salamanca quarter is informed throughout by its owner's philosophy of 'emotional intelligence'. Sobrino's sure hand, as much at ease with colour as with space, threads together the living- and working-areas to achieve a delicate balance between the two. In the confines of his small Madrileño apartment, he has fashioned a grand view of an equilibrium between human needs and desires, deploying cultures, spaces, shapes, lines and colours in a way that combines creative fantasy with a very real setting.

LEFT, TOP Black-and-white patterns in the living-area upholstery are echoed by the large and striking diptych painted by Sobrino.

LEFT, BOTTOM White ceramic candlesticks act as clean, bright exclamation marks amid a collection of bibelots.

OPPOSITE Watched over by a white marble bust of Alfonso XII, the luxuriously deep sofa is strewn with antique Indian textiles in black, white and fuchsia.

Vintage Retreat
Wine resort, Montserrat

Held in thrall to the riveting view of Catalunya's famous Montserrat peak, Can Bonastre Wine Resort extends an invitation to a lifestyle dominated by vine and glass. The solid stone-and-wood structure of the sixteenth-century *masia* underpins a present-day vision realized by the youngest of three generations: siblings Roger and Glòria Vallès have transformed their grandfather's agricultural property and their father's boutique winery into a modern haven of casual elegance.

Working with the Barcelona design firm Connecta, the owners established a common philosophy towards the renovation, based on the privileged setting of the original traditional Catalan farmhouse. Perched on a rocky outcrop in this wine-growing region half an hour from Barcelona, Can Bonastre overlooks the receding hills that lead to Montserrat, Catalunya's most famous geological icon. Connecta's brief was to design a five-star 'Grand Luxe' hotel inside a working winery. As the design company states: 'In its management of the project, Connecta has ensured that the architecture, landscaping and interior design are in complete harmony with the surroundings.'

The traditional *masia* sports a glow of *amarillo* (yellow) stucco, forming a gold cloak over the rambling sixteenth-century building that basks in the sun. A thoughtful approach to design unites the oldest loggia of the main house with the newest deluxe guest rooms, where the traditional ironwork balconies are echoed by modern *hierro labrado*, wrought-ironwork, in the form of vines. The relief effect of large blank

LEFT Outside two luxurious guest rooms, contemporary wrought-iron grape vines join original brick pillars and arches.

OPPOSITE A sentinel palm stands at the entrance to Can Bonastre's privileged setting overlooking Montserrat, the iconic geo-symbol of Catalunya.

stucco walls and further authentic original ironwork details at the entrance subtly prepare the visitor for the clean contemporary design used throughout the spacious *masia*.

Glòria Vallès greets guests at the entrance to the foyer, with its traditional brick-vaulted ceiling. The original massive oak, iron-nailed doors shield a set of silently gliding glass doors from the strong southern sun. Sheltered luminosity is a repeated motif throughout the building, as if the transparency provided by glass doors and walls, both etched and translucent, helps to define the vision created by the Vallès family.

The flow from hotel entrance to spa to winery to restaurant is deliberate and seamless. At the touch of a fingerpad, a glass wall melts into an arched brick opening to the Tribia restaurant. When viewed through the panoramic pool-level windows of the spa, the distant vision of Montserrat recedes as if it is a cutout silhouette. Nowhere is the sense of transparency more important than in the open lounge and viewing terrace, which capture all of Montserrat's glory in one long panoramic sweep of glass etched with the sierra's romantically named peaks. The Vallès siblings invite guests for an evening cocktail gathering as the mountain catches fire and then fades into violet and grey, under a full moon that leaves Can Bonastre to glow, itself a reflection of the gathered energy of the sun.

New technology complements traditional methods: nearly 50 per cent of the hot water for the beautifully conceived spa level is supplied by means of solar panels installed on the wine cellar's roof. Bathed in reflected light from Montserrat, a cascade of warm water agitates an iridescent-tiled pool. Reflections of light bounce from a sculpture of ovoid mirrors mounted on the mosaic ceiling, while light and shadow play in the walled-off corners constructed of native slate and stone. The Acbua

RIGHT, TOP AND BOTTOM The original carved door, set off with contemporary iron hardware, and the stone-and-iron staircase, now lit by a modern suspended lamp, exemplify the approach to mixing styles and periods in the historic building.

L SOL GROC, LA LLUM A

ADA SOLC, UN GEST AM

ADA CEP LI FA DE PATG

LES NITS LI DONEN CA

EL TURÓ DE CAN BONAST

E VI   YES, PAISA

spa at Can Bonastre recalls in miniature Connecta's meticulous design work with the Barcelona aquarium and other water-based clients.

Twelve guest rooms each feature a glass-walled bathroom etched with details from a topographical map of Montserrat's peaks and vales. South-facing rooms are screened from the sun with a solitary grand panel that disappears into the ceiling when a touchpad is pressed. The rooms marry traditional tiles and exotic-wood floors, Baroque frames and minimalist leather furniture; beds and walls are soberly coloured and clothed in deep velour and pebbled leather respectively, needing only the acid green or pure white of a contemporary chair or a hovering glass lamp as punctuation marks.

The attention to detail extends throughout: a high-tech humidifier in the barrel room, visible from the spa antechamber and panelled with a rust-patinated steel, hisses a gentle mist on cue; a wooden bucket in the spa echoes the wine barrels outside and provides a cooling splash for the sauna; the restaurant's smooth red-leather chairs are exactly the colour of a perfectly aged Nara, the winery's premium barrel-aged red wine. In fact, this precise shade of soft red is seen in various textures of tile, leather, velour and steel, serving as a subtle reminder of the resort's *raison d'être*.

Throughout, the feeling of modern luxury is decidedly young and contemporary, yet poised on a solid foundation of traditional materials. Oak doors, iron railings and stone floors reveal that this is, above all, a sixteenth-century home — one graciously converted for the visitor's pleasure. The delicate balance between hotel and home, new and old, soft and edgy, creates a sense of gentle contrast that greets guests of the Vallès family at the Can Bonastre Wine Resort.

LEFT, TOP AND BOTTOM Guest rooms feature recessed niches displaying individual natural sculptures as well as contemporary luxury bath fixtures.

OPPOSITE At ground level, the Acbua spa is a play of light and water on mosaic and polished stone, the reflections of which dance across the sun room, thanks to a hanging sculpture of circular mirrors.

City Style
Apartment, Madrid

From his Madrid-based boutique in the newly hip area of Chueca, Baruc Corazón, one of Spain's top young fashion designers, reinvents the classic button-down shirt while exalting a way of life that celebrates ease and style. As he states in a manifesto on design: 'TO BE ORIGINAL: to think, not copy. To search, not presume. All design should start from scratch, respecting its purpose, which is where its usefulness lies.' Nowhere is this manifesto more evident than in Corazón's own *pied-à-terre*, which combines, just as his fashion design does, a breezy style with a classic attention to detail.

Overlooking the Plaza Mayor in central Madrid, with its gridwork of light and dark paving, the balcony reveals a view of the arcaded square's pattern of shuttered French doors and iron balconies. The sweeping façades of rows and rows of apartments are lit by the sun as the hours pass from siesta to promenade; from here, too, one can watch the passing

LEFT, TOP Midday on the Plaza Mayor in Madrid, as seen from the balcony of clothing designer Baruc Corazón's apartment.

LEFT, BOTTOM Shuttered balconies shade the apartment.

OPPOSITE Extravagant painted murals adorn the façade of the Casa de la Panadería on the Plaza Mayor.

parade of Madrileños. The top floor, meanwhile, looks over the Baroque chaos of Madrid's rooftops and white wedding-cake façades, perhaps the inspiration for Corazón's own stylish contrast of organization and chaos. Within the confines of the classic structure, this apartment is a refreshing mix of personal expression and professional restraint.

With an elegant blend of contemporary and 1970s pop culture, Corazón creates a spare 'at home' stage set. A solitary spotlight on a long stem reaches to light a pair of leather chairs. 'My style doesn't change every six months,' says the designer. 'It matures and evolves, springing from my experiences, not from trends.' White walls and polished white floors serve as a backdrop to the carefully chosen furnishings. White runs through the apartment as a unifying note, allowing each small grouping of chairs, tables or photographs to catch the attention. Low fabric benches and a sofa square off, backs to the wall as if to stretch the compact space to its very edges, while a single carved wooden stool acts as a side-table.

When designing his timeless fashion solutions, Corazón restricts his fabric palette to classic colours, either in pinstripes (blue, charcoal and

In the sitting-room, a dramatic photograph, its impact heightened by simple lighting and the clean, spare lines of the surrounding furniture, takes centre stage.

beige) or in solids (blue, black and pink). At home, he readily embraces a more vibrant approach to pattern and colour. A glass-topped, chrome-tube table supporting a grouping of coloured-glass, teardrop vases is married to a chrome-and-wood chair; bright-red cushions punctuate the white couch; a verdant-green armchair stands against pristine white-painted woodwork alongside one of the designer's iconic new shirts.

The play of colours reaches its zenith in a graphically enhanced bedroom: orange, red and black brighten the white framework. Pop-art paintings, a hung folk-art quilt and the dizzying play of floral pattern in a bed-throw combine to create a space as personal as Corazón's philosophy of compatibility: 'I endeavour that all my pieces can be mixed and matched, that they are absolutely compatible with each other. Free. An intelligent piece of clothing is one that finds its pair, effortlessly.'

And so a stainless-steel cart wheels round, doubling as bar and desk beneath a gallery of sepia glamour portraits, while a cocky crystal chandelier lights the room. The kitchen trades off a standard stainless-steel front with a mirrored splashback and an informal gallery of art.

LEFT, TOP: Corazón happily mixes colours and styles to create a free and lively effect. Here, the impact of the black-and-chrome chairs contrasts with the softer look of sepia photographs.

LEFT, BOTTOM: Gleaming white walls offset vividly coloured furnishings, while display boxes of butterflies and dragonflies add interesting detail to the decor.

OPPOSITE: A cluster of teardrop vases in brilliant colours forms a dynamic contrast to the elegant restraint of the mirror immediately above.

'An intelligent item of clothing adapts itself to life, making it easier, not complicating it', Corazón explains. Whereas this manifesto might define his stylish and classical approach to dressing the public, from celebrities to eager fashionistas, his equally chic home is this city-dweller's casual solution to urban clutter. Just as Baruc Corazón has significantly reinterpreted the button-down shirt, so he bases his personal style in his central Madrid apartment on a strong, apparently uncontrived foundation, a contemporary mix of good design and personal flair.

A freewheeling mix of colours and patterns enlivens the high, white space of the bedroom and lends it a unique character.

Modernista Majesty
Seaside house, Cadaqués

Cadaqués, that whitewashed, blue-trimmed tumble of fishermen's houses and seaside retreats, wraps prettily round its protected bay on the Costa Brava. In a town full of simple stucco façades trimmed with washing-powder blue, Casa Blaua, the blue house, stands as the grande dame, a step above the slate-paved promenade. The owners, long-time residents of Cadaqués, purchased the house, which dates from the beginning of the twentieth century, in the 1980s, and faced the daunting task of returning it to its former glory as one of the most charming and accessible Catalan Modernista houses.

Casa Blaua towers well above the sea, its pristine white-and-blue tiled façade a fantasy of acanthus leaves and arabesques topped by a red steeple roof and a griffin weathervane that spins in the Mediterranean winds. Lateen-sailed fishing boats and modern yachts today run before the same winds that in the early twentieth century carried away numerous emigrants from Cadaqués to South America to seek their fortunes. Those returning newly wealthy were labelled 'Americanos' or 'Indianos', their risky adventures for gold and riches feted in song and dance. And so Casa Blaua is also called an Indiano, built by the architect Salvador Sellés i Baró in 1912 as a public display of success, and one of the last Modernista or art nouveau buildings in Catalunya inspired by the works of Antonio Gaudí. A student of Gaudí and a principal in building the Park Güell in Barcelona, Sellés asserted the status of the house's owners by means of gracefully

LEFT Cadaqués is famous for this view of its whitewashed façades of village houses, huddled beneath the spare exterior of the Church of Santa Maria, which conceals a magnificent Baroque altar.

OPPOSITE Casa Blaua's Modernista main building towers above the adjoining boathouse, which opens on to the harbour and stone-laid sea walls.

elegant, high-ceilinged salons and rooms opening to the morning sun reflected off the village's famous white church.

In a town of white stucco, blue shutters and red roofs, Casa Blaua is much admired for its exterior of enamelled tiles, both original and restored. Built on several levels as the village climbs the steep slate streets, the house is a warren of entrances and connecting staircases. Split by a steep passage, the entrance to the main building is protected from the high waters and the noise of the waterfront by a separate portside boathouse. On the harbour side, the curious, casual living-room, once the working boathouse of the villa, is the epitome of summer seaside living, a gathering-place for friends and family as well as a reflection of the lifestyle of this celebrated Catalan village. One exposed wall of stacked slate stone is evidence of the style of construction typical of this part of Catalunya. Indeed, thousands of miles of these same flat stones define the contours of entire hillsides, which descend to the village in dry-stone terraces built by the ancient occupants of the Cap Creus – Phoenicians, Greeks and Romans. At Casa Blaua, this one wall remains a testament to the hidden structure beneath the elegant mantle of smooth plaster and art nouveau tiles.

Having entered by the boathouse, one arrives in the main building via stairs and alleyways that connect terraces with the street level. Once the water-cistern and olive-oil storage level, the first floor invites the contemporary guest to leave the casual seaside ambience behind and assume the elegance of another time. Casa Blaua strikes a balance between preserving the glories and grandeur of the past and celebrating the informal, international artistic lifestyle for which Cadaqués is now famous. The spare yet Baroque furnishings of the large, elegantly

OPPOSITE In the boathouse, blue and white woodwork and walls reflect the sea, while a bare stone wall reveals the essential structure of the building.

RIGHT Stairs lead from the boathouse to an elevated connecting terrace and another entrance at street level.

proportioned rooms lend them a modern if slightly elaborate air, underscored by the casual throwing-open of the floor-to-ceiling doors and shutters to the clear Mediterranean air.

Dozens of doors connect or sequester spaces and, left ajar, invite the eye to flow from one level to the next. The principal door to the second floor displays a curious juxtaposition of new, industrial-age details and old-world elements. With a design as economical and beautiful as any in present-day trends, the original chrome hardware has been specially engineered to fasten a triple layer of shutters, glass, and wooden doors against the intemperate winter storms. And while a collection of Murano crystal chandeliers pays homage to the current owner's Italian origins, many of the other lights and bathroom fixtures and fittings date from the original construction of 1912 and are still in use.

A colourful tiled frieze rims the central salon, which separates a formal dining-room and an informal music salon. The *baldosas hidráulicas* – original patterned cement tiles first celebrated by Gaudí in many of his own residences – form a unifying mosaic of muted grey and cream on this level. These tiles, still manufactured in Spain using nineteenth-century techniques, were considered a more elegant alternative to the traditional local terracotta floor-tiles seen in less exalted period residences. Here they provide a visual link between the passageways and sitting-rooms, and an optical anchor for the hand-painted plasterwork on the lofty ceilings.

This generously proportioned, gracious living-level opens out on to a terrace perched over a public passageway between the boathouse and the villa, enabling the owners and their guests to become as much a part of the traditional evening promenade as the strollers on the waterfront below. From here, the town of Cadaqués can be admired glorying in the changing colours and shadows as the sun sets behind the sheltering hill.

RIGHT, TOP AND BOTTOM The main entrance to the first-floor living-quarters is via a tiled and ironwork staircase and an ornately appointed foyer featuring original lighting fixtures and chrome door hardware.

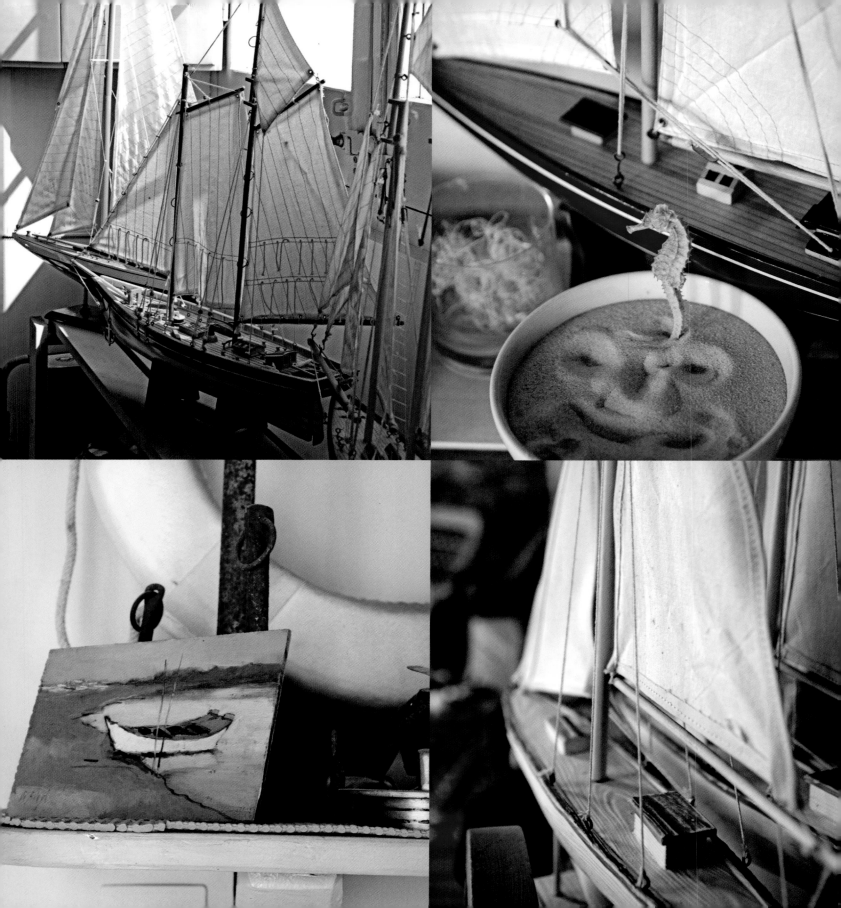

These views of Cadaqués, little changed from the earliest photographs and paintings of the village that were created by such artists as Salvador Dalí, Pablo Picasso, Joan Miró and Marcel Duchamp, who famously used to frequent the place, are mirrored in an important collection of paintings by contemporary artist Shigeyoshi Koyama, depicting Cadaqués from the 1970s to the present day. A muted echo of the external vistas, they present a sober graphic interpretation of the setting in which Casa Blaua dominates, a solid part of the village's scenery and cultural history.

The house's privileged setting allows the bay's luminosity to flood into the upper bedroom, as simple in its blue walls and cement-tile floors as a modern loft. The spare furnishings of the single bathroom and adjoining lavatory focus attention on the original decorative fixtures – lamps, doorknobs, drains and taps – that, now restored and in working order, enhance the architect's Modernista style with what was, for its time, an innovative approach to form and function.

Built towards the end of an extraordinary era of art nouveau design, the renovated Casa Blaua melds the romantic past of Cadaqués with a current vision of coastal living that encompasses both architectural decoration and the native character of a place. Although exuding the sophisticated insouciance of a seaside folly, this ornate and majestic home typifies the exuberance that the Catalan Modernista movement defined, which represented a reawakening of the Catalan national character. In so doing, it displays another dramatic facet of Spanish style.

LEFT, TOP Details of etched and leaded glass and elaborate tilework celebrate the Catalan Modernista period, defined by the work of Antonio Gaudí and his followers.

LEFT, BOTTOM Sea light bounces off the patterned cement tiles that were favoured during the twentieth century, and floods a blue-washed guest room furnished with the bare essentials – bed, table and armoire.

OPPOSITE Towering blue doors open and close off bedrooms, bathroom and toilet on the sleeping-level.

Contemporary Andalucía

Private home, Sotogrande

Defining contemporary Spanish design is as tricky as defining what makes Spanish cuisine distinctive. Is it the ingredients – the prized Iberian *jamón*, the peppery olive oil and the regional wines – or such techniques as grilling *ala plancha* or cooking in a terracotta *cazuela*? More likely, a singular individual dish evokes a season or a region and pronounces, 'This is Spain!' Similarly with contemporary Spanish design: is it the traditional materials and craftsmanship, or a way of looking at the world from the Iberian peninsula, that defines Spanish style?

The houses on which interior designer Thomas Urquijo puts his distinctive stamp are as internationally Spanish as he is, the epitome of what is now called the 'New European'. Urquijo, raised in Paris and schooled in London, now lives in Madrid, and combines these different cultural elements with a deft hand. He involves himself in all aspects of a project, contributing to every ingredient in a house design, from the initial stages, working alongside the architect, to the polished details of the finished building. Here in Andalucía, near the exclusive residential resort of Las Cimas near Sotogrande, Urquijo has created a private weekend home for a Madrid owner. Overlooking vistas of land and sea, the house, tucked into a private gated community, benefits from its privileged location.

LEFT, TOP Natural wood weathers to a soft grey in the strong southern sun softening the deck, its terrace awning and poolside lounge chairs.

LEFT, BOTTOM Pale-gold stone stairs climb to a rooftop terrace and barbecue area.

OPPOSITE The pool and sun terrace are set a step down from the ground-floor level and overlook the rolling hills and the Mediterranean Sea near Gibraltar.

'I propose creations with various views in mind and wait for the surprises', says Urquijo – and here, the surprising play of landscape and interior begins as soon as one enters through a simple iron gate.

The soaring entrance courtyard signals the beginning of this oasis of good design, where a sentinel palm stands under a rippled blue-and-white sky. At once garden and room, the space is defined by cubic niches and palm shadows, with the playful inclusion of a game of giant wooden balls; orange enamelled tables are a modern nod to Andalucía's Moorish influence. A narrow fall of water descends from a contemporary bronze cog, splashing down the stucco walls into a stone basin. The wind, kept out at wall height, rattles in the palm fronds, echoing the sound of falling water as it sings against the stone. This is the quintessential Spanish courtyard at its sparest – one tree, one fountain, one door leading to the interior of the house.

Behind the massive wooden entrance door, light filters through many gauze-draped windows that act both as a shelter from the strong sun and as an invitation to gaze out towards the distant Mediterranean Sea. Whereas the exterior is a tight play on niches and flat planes, the interior of the three-bedroom house is as luxurious as a private hotel in its attention to texture and detail. With a controlled and controlling hand, Urquijo orchestrates the many lavish furnishing details provided by his studio artists and craftspeople. Elements as diverse as art deco allusions, in a mirror frame with a faux-ivory finish, and Berber embroidered cushions, marry in easy elegance in these bright and spacious rooms.

Populated with precisely chosen furnishings more often than not designed by Urquijo himself, the ordered roles of salon, dining-rooms and guest rooms are cleverly defined by the designer's subtle palette. Room by room, Urquijo's commitment to surprise is underlined by delightful

RIGHT A sheet of water, a spare version of traditional Andalucían courtyard fountains, runs down the stone wall that shelters the informal outside dining-area.

artefacts and discoveries, such as a pair of jade discs in the guest sitting-room, a couple of mid-twentieth-century Murano glass vases in the master bedroom, and a dining-set of coral-red lacquerware waiting behind a wall of mirrors and forged iron. That Urquijo is a stickler for delicious detail in colour and material is visible in the way that, for example, grosgrain ribbon is sewn on to more ribbon until the weight of colour, line and fabric is in perfect harmony on a wall of gossamer linen drapery.

The designer took advantage of the open flow of spaces created by architect Pablo Carvajal, which immediately draws one into a capacious main salon generously squared around a large blond table under a cut-out bronze-and-glass chandelier. Unifying a celebration of Moorish designs as spare as one can find in Andalucía, a calm cream-and-brown palette decorates a riot of textiles that cover canapé sofas and fat club chairs as well as hand-embroidered Moroccan cushions.

Throughout the salon, Urquijo chooses a matt-finished, putty-coloured plaster to glaze the walls and serve as a neutral support for his collection of favoured faux finishes — cracked eggshell, vellum and aged ivory — against which he places fine red-lacquer tables and earthy iron-oxide ceramic vases. Large bronze bowls and vases lend additional weight to an otherwise ethereal pair of graceful standing lamps, each of which bears a solitary glass teardrop dangling like an oversized earring.

Berber-inspired heavy woven curtains, striped with rich brown, tobacco, coffee and cream, separate the main salon from a second sitting-area, awash with soft light from a wall of windows. The revealing contrast between indoors and outdoors returns in this room, as a gentle luminosity, filtering through the gauze-hung windows, fills the space, while elsewhere in the room, more windows, intricately patterned with dark wood, frame the wide, sunlit panorama beyond. Urquijo chooses blackened wood for a pair of *chaises longues*, upholstered with striped wool fabric, and a

A neutral palette of cream, ecru and deep brown is enriched by a broad use of texture in the serene and softly lit salon.

collection of stools, tables and benches on which to perch. Tribal designs echo in these strong sculptural pieces, reinforced by a collection of theatrical ethnic jewellery and hammered-silver shells.

A duo of dining-areas continues the interior–exterior game. A vast circle of polished wood inside has as its counterpart a square stone table on the outside dining-terrace. Each has its appeal as the sun crosses overhead and casts shadows or reflections into the mirrored formal dining-room. While a wall of water cascades gently outside, inside, a solitary crystal ball, suspended from a stunning circular bronze lamp, throws light on to the gridwork of mirrored surfaces that conceals the dining-service and reflects the view. A pair of painted, faux-vellum pillars supports two giant clam shells that act as reflectors, directing columns of soft light to the ceiling.

In this house set under the strong Andalucían sun, the effects of dark wood and strong design are softened as one mounts the pristine staircase built of local stone. A single teardrop of molten glass lights the way to a sitting-room that is the focus for the two guest rooms and the master suite. On this level, the softest of colours, and pristine white, create a restful haven. A washed-aqua-blue linen weave covers both armchairs and ottomans placed before a bookshelf of tobacco-stained oak. The twin guest rooms overlook the green fields to the sea view, while the master bedroom turns away to the hills.

OPPOSITE Reflected in iron-framed mirror doors that conceal china and linens stored behind them, the custom-made circular pedestal dining-table and -chairs continue the monochromatic scheme.

RIGHT, TOP The original design of the bold bronze cylinder chandelier evokes the natural materials that Urquijo favours for this weekend retreat.

RIGHT, BOTTOM One of a pair of columns, finished in faux vellum, which supports a natural shell concealing a spotlight that gently illuminates the room as evening falls.

Painted in a soft, warm grey, the master suite is a sanctuary of pale eau-de-Nil green fabric. The gently curving fern spirals that pattern the curtains are echoed in the delicate carving of the silver wooden headboard; Italian reading-lamps are set on immaculate small grey chests that host hidden drawers for bedside needs. A solitary note of red — an enamelled plate resting on a bronze table — offsets the delicate velour reading-seat. Once again, Urquijo makes a bold statement with dark wooden bookcases, similar to those used elsewhere in the house, this time softened by the shape of oversized carved wooden 'pebbles' supporting the shelves. The custom-woven rug and immaculate white linens soften the effect of the stone-tiled floors that link all the bedrooms.

In one guest room, a creamy leather chaise matches the floor stone, while heavy cream-and-red curtains fall over red-striped gauzy linen. More red is seen on the beautiful lacquer stools sitting at the foot of the four-poster beds. This is where Urquijo's passion for texture shines through, in his choice of a large round art deco mirror painted to resemble an eggshell ivory-and-nacre (mother-of-pearl) mosaic and lit by thick lithographic paper-shaded lamps on matching varnished blond tables. The other guest room harmonizes soft-green benches, dark headboards and pristine linens with a deep, intense blue, showing off its cooler face to the distant sea.

Here, in this chic neighbourhood in Andalucía's coastal hills, Thomas Urquijo gathers a tasteful display of international influence under his skilful hand. The final effect is decidedly Spanish — a celebration of light and shade, texture and colour that plays off the landscape near the Mediterranean Sea with an interior motif of delight and surprise.

LEFT, TOP AND BOTTOM Twin guest rooms reflect the serene style created by impeccable linens and well-chosen furnishings.

OPPOSITE The master bedroom is a spare yet somehow opulent haven of soft-green silk fabric and silver-stained wood, with finishing touches in faux ivory.

New Farmhouse Style
Weekend home, Casavells

This eighteenth-century stone *masia* belonging to Catalan gallery owner Miquel Alzueta sits solidly on a rocky flank above the rural landscape of the Baix Empordá region of northern Catalunya. A casual filigree of old olive-trees, oaks and figs, cherries, juniper, and grape vines screens an otherwise unfettered view of the Mediterranean Sea. The stone bones of this country home are 100 per cent Catalan *rústica*. Alzueta bought this farmhouse, previously owned by the same family for five generations and relatively untouched, and transformed it into a retreat, near his country gallery in the medieval village of Casavells.

The house, with its thick stone walls, nestles into a gentle hill. The ground floor undulates with the natural rise and fall of the monolithic slab that thus serves as a foundation of varying levels. A swimming pool provides relief from the summer heat; beside it, a natural pond serves to catch and store the seasonal rains for garden use. Here, the house turns its back to the strong afternoon sun and casts its own shadow across the terrace and gardens.

Another shadow, thrown by a graceful arc of iron and reeds, marries the two completely independent living-areas, which, at weekends, are shared by Alzueta and his daughter's family. A traditional reed covering waits for young wisteria and jasmine vines to bridge the family guest house and the main house, and shade the long, narrow table used for family gatherings. Two separate kitchens serve the central courtyard

LEFT The sunny setting for the terracotta-tiled swimming pool looks out towards the Mediterranean Sea.

OPPOSITE Behind its textured stone exterior, the eighteenth-century farmhouse harbours a gallery owner's collection of painted furniture.

for casual dining — a courtyard that forms the core of what is both a family country home and a bachelor's quiet retreat.

As a contemporary art and antiques dealer, Alzueta particularly enjoys the mix of old and new. Playing the strict, old, stone structure against artful industrial furnishings, he has created a dramatic tension between up-to-date art and salvaged metal furniture. Low Catalan vaulted ceilings, built with rush and stone, arch above polished cement floors. Smooth white plaster walls form a backdrop to Alzueta's anthology of carefully chosen metal furnishings.

The first glimpse of this quirky collection is a metal garden bench striped by layers and layers of gently eroded paint that reveal contrasting colours like stories of past lives. Simple woven rugs thrown throughout the house echo the striped patterns, while two ancient Adirondack chairs, with bleached-grey wood grain and faded white paint, continue the play of texture and basic materials.

OPPOSITE A canopy of woven reeds throws textured shadows across a shared outdoor dining-area bridging the two living-spaces.

ABOVE The east-facing side of the house opens on to a casual garden landscaped with fig, olive and lavender.

Once the entrance to the stables, the foyer descends at the same gentle angle as the slope on which it is built, into the other ground-floor rooms. A pair of old glass-paned doors ushers one into a cloakroom; another door leads to an intimate dining-area. From a third door, the deep blue of a long, vaulted kitchen beckons.

The kitchen is a study in simplicity. A school-room table and benches, revealing their previous green, yellow and tangerine incarnations, hint at the simple lifestyle that the *masia* extols. A functional, unbroken counter of stainless steel runs down one side of the long, narrow room, housing stove, sink and storage. The original fireplace, blackened by winter use and guarded by a pair of winking sphinxes, anchors the kitchen to its ancient roots. The silver counter reflects light back from a solitary window on to a mottled blue plaster wall – that particular washing-powder blue used throughout Catalunya. A stippled blue jug holds the colour note here, while a surprising retro-modern touch – a sparkling-pink 1950s-style refrigerator – faces a faded-red metal cabinet that serves as a crockery cupboard. Local terracotta squares, raw-finished, tile the floor, a simple solution for a summer house for family and friends.

The interior stone path leads on down to a snug dining-room sheltered from the early-morning sun by thick stone walls. The room is dominated by a red-and-white rectangular contemporary painting, and a faded-red metal lamp hovers like a 1960s spaceship over the circular table. Alzueta's industrial-fixtures collection features a former carpentry workbench

OPPOSITE Throughout the house, from the master bathroom to the library to the guest kitchen, gridworks of frames and shelves unify a diverse collection of material.

RIGHT, TOP AND BOTTOM Interior doors open on to living-areas connected by polished cement floors that play off rough-textured vaulting with stone-and-plaster walls.

serving as a sideboard. Against a backdrop of smooth, raw-plaster walls, each steel object – table, chairs, lamps – textured by age, displays a myriad colours worn away to reveal the dark, oxidized metal beneath. The juxtaposition of colour and steel against limewash lightens the heavy look of these undomestic but industrially beautiful fixtures.

The flow of small, connected spaces leads to the main sitting-room, tucked into the back of the house, a quiet retreat from the outside world. This comfortable room, with its warm grey walls, invites gentle repose on a pair of charcoal velour settees, while a trio of sober eighteenth- and nineteenth-century portraits of ladies and gentlemen looks on. The calm atmosphere of a winter sitting-room centres round the well-used fireplace sporting a classical wooden dentil mantlepiece. A quirky rustic menagerie of wood, cement and pottery sculptures – ducks, swans, geese, sheep – keeps company with the tigers, elephants and long-necked deer bounding underfoot along a charming Persian rug.

That this is a masculine domain is nowhere more evident than in Alzueta's simple solution to curtains. Made from men's shirting material – blue, white or charcoal pinstripes – they are draped chemise-width lengths over simple iron rods: a tug of fabric suffices to block the sun. Large white porcelain urns and natural linen complement the simple elegance of this space, Alzueta's private chamber.

Upstairs, the play of strong colour and materials continues. The master bedroom features a simple platform of found wood for an oversized bed

LEFT, TOP AND BOTTOM Miquel Alzueta's private collection of battered 'found objects' is displayed as precisely as his gallery selections.

OPPOSITE An industrial metal suspension lamp hovers over a bare metal circular table in the dining-room, which is dominated by a contemporary painting by Catalan artist Miquel Mont.

with its singularly large pillow. Deep-green metal panels function as both headboard and artwork, while two favourite paintings hang at pillow height, an intimate bedside touch. Reflected in a well-placed mirror, the unexpected contrast of an aqua-blue Baroque desk next to a solid-steel armoire teases the eye. Here, too, charcoal-pinstriped shirting frames both a simple square fireplace and a window giving wonderful views to the coastal hills. The first morning sun warms the natural terracotta tiles that flow out on to an elevated private rooftop terrace, the owner's quiet tree-height retreat.

Elsewhere on the second floor, blue walls soften a double guest room and recall the blue kitchen below. The large wooden desk and chair, also painted a sea-blue colour, focus attention on a gallery of precious small artworks on paper. This is a spacious room, in which light filtering in through a single window shines on bedclothes of coarse white linen and silky embroidered pillowcases. The same rough-hewn wood that was used in the master bedroom serves here for side-tables and bed-frame; two old fishing-boat rudders act as a headboard.

Next door, a delicate twin guest room slumbers in deep-yellow shadow. Two simple beds, separated by a wide iron table, are watched over by more nineteenth-century portraits. This dim light is typical in these old stone houses, where curtains are drawn severely against the brilliant sun. Alzueta pays particular attention to lighting these rooms. Here, a contemporary floor lamp acts as a modern punctuation mark to the

OPPOSITE The original spartan, blue-washed colour scheme in the kitchen is punctuated by a retro note of pink that echoes the raw-finished terracotta-tile floor.

RIGHT, TOP A friendly menagerie of animal sculptures gathers around a charcoal velour settee in the owner's private living-space.

RIGHT, BOTTOM Layers of red and white paint on an iron park bench set the colour theme and textures for the entrance room, presided over by an anonymous portrait of a lady in a red shawl.

dark-painted armoire full of freshly ironed linens and the floor of patterned Modernista cement tiles.

Like the bedrooms, the library faces east, to where the morning sun rises over the Mediterranean. The light of the not-so-distant sea invades the room and illuminates a wall of wooden boxes that serve as bookshelves, and a conservationist's homage to the nearby wetlands – a flock of stuffed rare birds, preserved in nature boxes.

In the pools of light and shadow thrown by a red bowl-shaped lamp, twin to one in the dining-room below, stand a well-scrubbed gateleg table, a leather club chair and two old French garden tables. Powder-pink matt terracotta tiles provide a suitably muted flooring in this upstairs haven of quiet, where it seems as if the click of footsteps might wake the perched birds.

Back outside, in the bright afternoon light and across the connecting terrace, the family guest house displays its palette of cool blue-grey and lava-grey stone, creamy cement and oxidized-red metal. These faded colours of paint layers and basic materials are softened further, inside, by printed bedlinens and pillows. Quirky industrial ware, such as a French parachute locker used as a kitchen cupboard, and a roll-down iron armoire from a garage, provides a link with the other side of the house.

Miquel Alzueta has lightened the weight of his eighteenth-century stone house, now delicately balanced through elegant design, with a singular collection of industrial-strength furniture and contemporary art. His home – unlike those of many gallery owners – remains a very private retreat, while at the same time inviting the visitor to browse his galleries in Barcelona and Casavells for inspired treasures similar to those they discover here.

With its metal headboard and 'found-wood' platform, the master bedroom has a low centre of gravity that counterpoises the lofty slanted ceiling.

Collector's Idyll

Apartment, Madrid

On a wide, white corner of one of Madrid's exclusive residential quarters, a dynamic second-floor family home combines the rigorous requirements of art collectors and the casual city lifestyle of a young urban family. Briefed to unify two apartments, Madrid-based designer Borja Azcarate was given a free hand by his clients to demolish, restore and enhance. The now-expanded home must both serve casual family activities and display the formal contemporary elegance demanded by an outstanding international collection of twentieth-century paintings and photographs.

Azcarate's first act was to transform the foyer into a generous entrance, which became a true gallery once the ceilings were taken down and the space opened out and up. As in the rest of the large apartment, the play of old and new, refined and industrial creates a dynamic structure on which to hang the owner's favourite works from an extensive private collection. The 4-metre-long (13 feet) industrial iron table, sourced from a Catalan machine shop, fills the large gallery, contrasting with a warm, polished parquet of honey-coloured pine that itself seems to glide across the entrance floor.

All other rooms and corridors spin out from this central art-filled foyer: children's rooms, kitchen and casual living in one direction; the

LEFT A hanging zinc clock keeps time at the entrance to the grey-and-cream-coloured kitchen area.

OPPOSITE A deep, plush velour sofa and a custom-built iron-and-ceramic table furnish the more formal sitting-room of this urbane Madrid apartment.

OPPOSITE Towering metal bookcases stand at regular
intervals around the edge of this area dedicated to
reading and family activities. The room is lit by a tin
chandelier, which is reflected in the sculptures sitting
on the mirrored tabletop.

ABOVE The door between the sitting-room and the
entrance-foyer gallery is framed by twin Directoire tables.

master bedroom suite with private sitting-room and two bathrooms in
another; a corner library/entertaining-room, formal living-room and dining-
area in yet another. Azcarate transformed small, dull rooms throughout the
apartment by restoring the intricate decorative plaster ceiling and cornice
work, thereby lifting the eye to the original three-metre (10-foot) ceiling
height. Fibre-optic lights hidden behind decorative elements pick out the
carved details and create a soft glow that reflects the pure-white ceiling
on to richly coloured furnishings and the contemporary art beneath.

The large apartment wraps round the corner building, the sun tracking
the hours and lighting each window in turn. In the main salon, original
crystal-paned leaded windows cast the Spanish red-and-yellow flag on to
a pair of 1950s American armchairs as the sun sweeps past. Deep-seated
modern ball-and-claw sofas face each other, their charcoal velour
complementing an iron-framed table created specially for the space.

A pair of Directoire tables, with a red-lacquered, faux-marble finish, frames the entrance door and contributes to the stable and well-balanced atmosphere of the room. The intricate marquetry parquet, uncovered and refinished to a warm glow, anchors the different periods on a classic foundation.

Asked to design a space fit for entertaining, Azcarate created a dramatic dining-room that doubles as a showcase for the largest of the abstract paintings. Walls were papered in 1-metre (3¼-foot) squares of a smooth Geotextil fabric called veloglass, a modern-day alternative to vellum, and then painted a light-absorbing black, which softens the effect of the bold colours and high ceilings. Convex mirrors balance two large glass-topped, brass square tables that Azcarate designed especially for the space. Inspired by the early twentieth-century French designer Jean-Michel Frank's signature use of shagreen (textured sharkskin) on furniture, Azcarate

ABOVE The oversized entrance, dominated by an industrial iron table, connects all the living-areas of the apartment and serves its art-collecting owners as a formal gallery.

OPPOSITE Two contemporary paintings by Julian Opie hang either side of the leaded-glass sitting-room door.

designed the chairs using customized leather upholstery from his family's leatherworks. Two grand crystal chandeliers that once hung in a Madrid theatre and were found abandoned in Bilbao have been salvaged and now hover above the dramatic formal arrangement of furniture and space, uniting it into a comfortable dining- and entertaining-room for twelve.

The two children's rooms extend off the hall, closed off for privacy by a door, above which flickers a Jenny Holzer neon word-sculpture. In the boy's room, a plaster-and-wood headboard, masquerading as concrete and topped with oversized letters, dominates the seriously male photographs of city cars and garages on the walls and ceiling, while an original Arne Jacobsen leather *Egg* chair dominates a comfortable reading corner. The girl's room, with a chinoiserie theme, centres round a large crystal chandelier painted matt white to mimic the carved-plaster finish on the ceiling. Below it, twin black wooden bed-frames define the personal space.

The master suite, sequestered behind traditional shutters and curtains, is papered in the faux-vellum finish and painted ivory, the restful, filtered light making the room a haven of calm. Oiled pine floors and a simple wooden headboard balance the industrial television stand designed by Azcarate, while a feminine sofa, rescued from the flea market in Paris, complements the Robert Allen fabrics in the rest of the room. 'His' bathroom is white-and-grey Carrara marble; 'hers' is filled with black Marquina marble rising from a black-painted wooden floor.

The lofty library is the place where the family gathers together to listen to music or watch television, and features walls of iron bookcases

LEFT, TOP AND BOTTOM Two of Azcarate's distinctive convex mirrors reflect examples of the owner's colourful collection of contemporary art.

OPPOSITE Black, vellum-like walls absorb the fractured light cast by a pair of crystal chandeliers in the formal dining-room. Beneath the chandeliers stand two Azcarate-designed glass-topped brass tables.

designed by Azcarate to play off a dark-tin chandelier. The pine herringbone parquet supports dark-leather club chairs and sofas arranged informally around an antique mirror sign set into a custom-designed iron table from Azcarate's own collection.

The muted tones used throughout the apartment continue into the hidden kitchen, with its floor laid with a harlequin pattern of cream and charcoal tiles. A zinc table stands in the centre; industrial galvanized shelving, fitted with elegant glass doors, houses the refined silver service – a wonderful play of old and new, raw and finished.

While Azcarate's judicious hand is evident in every detail throughout this exquisite family home, he never masks the personality and purpose of the owner's family or art collection. His signature design work, most evident in the custom-made furniture, reflects his precise and controlled approach, assembling the elements that create at once a comfortable urban family home and a showcase for a serious art collection. Azcarate easily incorporates a new international layer of design and art with the solid foundation of classic Spanish style and craftsmanship.

OPPOSITE, TOP Black marble and glass have been combined to create a luxurious bathroom, lit by standing lamps and ceiling fixtures.

OPPOSITE, BOTTOM LEFT Zinc and galvanized metal unify the spare kitchen surfaces, while industrial shelving has been modified to house wine, crystal and fine silver.

OPPOSITE, BOTTOM RIGHT The black Marquina marble of the art deco-style guest bathroom is reflected in a chrome-finished mirror.

RIGHT, TOP An original Arne Jacobsen *Egg* chair in camel-coloured leather stands in contrast to the faux-concrete-finished headboard in the boy's bedroom.

RIGHT, BOTTOM The sitting-area off the master suite is a relaxed and open contemporary space used by the entire family.

Informal Elegance
Private home and antique showcase, Baix Empordà

What does a designer and restorer of old houses do when he falls in love with a view from a stable? The solution for Serge Castella was to convince his partner, Jason Flinn, to move their prize Appaloosa horses to a new, larger setting and convert the original stables into a modern country loft.

After restoring several old Catalan houses in the area, Castella and Flinn knew what to keep of the old and how to make it fresh. Castella remembers, 'We'd find an old house, make it beautiful and then sell it.' They were living in the last of these restored old farmhouses, where they had built a stable and hayloft to house their Appaloosas ten years before. 'We wanted a more open space; easy and more comfortable. We loved the location here, with the view of the field. It faces east; the south is too hot here in the Baix Empordà.' Deciding to sell the house and keep the stables, they approached the challenge with their eyes open. Creating an understated backdrop for a revolving collection of beautiful antique and contemporary pieces, this antiques dealer and designer transformed a basic farm building into a comfortable home and casual showroom.

Under a traditional ceiling of timber rafters, and unified by the treatment of the interior walls, the living- and office areas are well lit by a wall of glass doors.

Castella's and Flinn's clients, whether for antiques or horses, come to visit as much for the lifestyle as for business. The property is reached after a cautious ride down a rough dirt track, through the open fields and wildflower-strewn landscapes of rural Catalunya. Two large, symmetrical, oval windows flank a double door that leads from the large gravel parking area into a generous open quadrangle, the modest origins of which are quickly forgotten.

Neither contrived nor careless, two bedrooms and two bathrooms secure each end of the large open rectangle. At just 175 square metres (1880 sq. feet) in total, the rest of the house is divided into three distinct areas – kitchen and dining, living-room, and office. Castella chose a single unifying treatment for both exterior and interior walls throughout. White cement and beige sand combine to cover all the vertical surfaces and form a backdrop to modern art and antique alike. Castella explains, 'We didn't want white. That is the colour of the sea, like at Cadaqués [Castella is referring here to the all-white buildings in the seaside town]. This local sand is of the earth – a rich earth colour, very restful.' Lofty ceilings are plastered white and lighten the look of the heavy traditional *viga* (roof-rafter) timbers.

OPPOSITE The sand-coloured walls of the former stables provide a rich yet neutral background for simple garden furnishings and native plants.

RIGHT, TOP AND BOTTOM Outside, iron and terracotta details provide textured relief against the simple earth- and stone-coloured backdrops.

The warm sand background is a perfect textural foil for a rotating show of art. Fine-grained wide planks support the elegantly wrought legs of a Giacometti coffee-table one month, a low Chinese chest the next; each visit finds a new piece from Castella's on-site showroom of things he loves. The bleached-oak floors, sourced from Belgium over the Internet, run throughout the home and soften the steps that move from terrace to stable. Castella recalls, 'We didn't make a plan; one day the builder said, "Now we need a floor", and so we found it.'

The entire home flows from one open space into the next. A simple system of partial walls separates the office from the sitting-area, where, in turn, a facing fireplace forms a boundary to the rest of the space, which is used as a large kitchen. The eastern wall opens to the outside through large, grid-worked glass doors and floods the carefully chosen tribal art or cherished antiques with a flattering morning light.

Castella has gathered the kitchen together with a lovely old painted wooden buffet and a simple trestle table offsetting a stark stainless-steel work surface, on which is displayed a personal collection of corals and shells. A recent acquisition – *Skull and Volcano* – by the late Bernard Buffet now takes the place of honour over the centre fireplace in the

OPPOSITE A lithograph by Bernard Buffet graces the fireplace mantle in the central living-room.

RIGHT, TOP AND BOTTOM Two opposite corners of the open office that serves to house Castella's art collection.

sitting-area. Each decorative touch of sculpture or natural objects is delicately balanced by open space and invites closer examination of a collection of favourite treasures.

As in the rest of the house, the master suite is a simple palette of neutrals, this time broken only by the rich pewter-coloured bedcover. A traditional Catalan painted door closes a bathroom armoire, while another door — this time from the Piedmont in Italy — with its wooden shelf built into the frame, displays yet more treasures. And while Castella's carefully chosen stock rotates through the house, his personal possessions — a William Wegman photograph over the bed, an anonymous bronze bust, a white plaster lamp — confirm his love of eclectic styles.

Castella carefully assembles the pieces that have transformed the stable into a modern adaptation of a classic country home — spacious, inviting and open to the landscape. In this sunlit, informal region that encourages outside living as much as inside entertaining, the sparse surroundings are enticement enough. Old French iron garden furniture and artfully ranged terracotta pots are sufficient decoration on this generous gravel canvas. The large glass wall opens on to a garden of santolina, an aromatic shrub, a solitary patch punctuated with olive-trees, and the open field that encouraged Castella and Flinn to stay. Castella muses as he remembers the other houses they have made beautiful, and then admits: 'This is the house I'd like to keep.'

OPPOSITE A stainless-steel worktop unites the utilitarian kitchen and is softened with natural material, such as basketry, wood and coral.

RIGHT, TOP All of the kitchen appliances and fittings flow along one side of the room.

RIGHT, BOTTOM A woven Catalan market basket fills the gap in the summer fireplace.

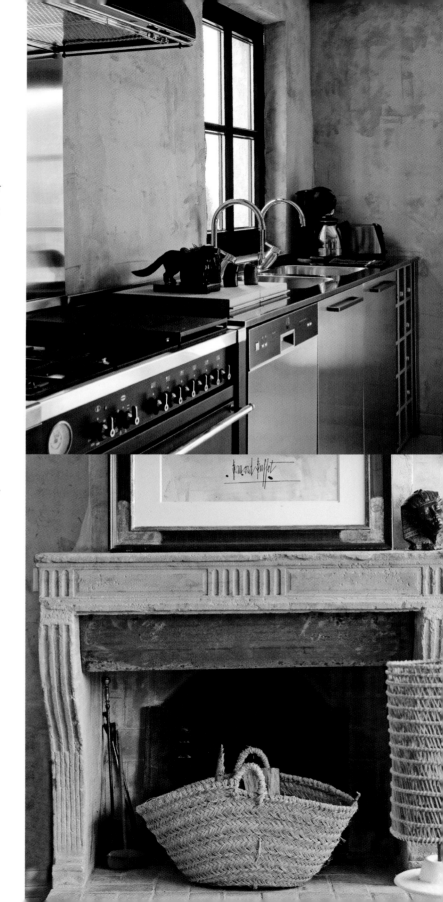

Historic Hospitality

Parador hotel, Santiago de Compostela

The cross of St James is etched on every glass door of the Hostal dos Reis Católicos, the exemplary parador in Santiago de Compostela in Galicia. As if travellers might need a reminder that they have reached the end of the long, historic pilgrims' road, the spiritual logo of the cross appears in courtyard boxwood topiary, woven into deep plush carpets, embroidered with fine gold thread, watermark-stencilled on painted walls, and carved in stone. Considered to be the world's oldest hotel, the Royal Hospital was established as a pilgrims' hospice in 1499; history told in stone, a calm, centuries-old presence, it sits on the Plaza do Obradoiro, near Santiago's Baroque towered cathedral.

From medieval times, the grand building offered shelter to weary travellers from northern European homelands and elsewhere who had walked the many dangerous miles of the pilgrimage route, the Way of St James. Today's pilgrims often share the road with more secular tourists, and the parador at Santiago gathers all into its sturdy granite arms with a gracious hospitality born of five hundred years of offering welcome, rest and solace.

The stacked-granite fabric of the building becomes dark and shiny in the Galician prevailing weather – rain. Locals continually remind you that 'to see Santiago, you must have rain', and 'Santiago is more beautiful in

LEFT, TOP AND BOTTOM The western façade of the Cathedral of Santiago de Compostela faces the Plaza del Obradoiro and features a magnificent staircase ascending to the late-Baroque entrance.

OPPOSITE One of four interior courtyards of the parador. The clipped boxwood hedges represent the royal crown and cross of St James.

the rain.' Umbrellas are flourished, and the sound of water spewing from ghoulish gargoyles echoes off the stone court. Here, graceful arches offer shelter from the rain, rather than from the hot sun as in southern Andalucía.

A cross-shaped chapel divides the austere granite block into four courtyards honouring the four gospels. In one courtyard, a low boxwood hedge, clipped into the shapes of a crown and a cross, is another reminder of the past. In its centre, a stone-topped wishing-well dripping in the rain competes with the music of coins as pilgrims arrive at their destination. In another, fountains and wells, gargoyles and discreet carved gutters speak of abundant water. The elements of stone and water lie at the very foundations of this inn.

The San Lucas square leads past the chapel itself and through the 'death door', with its overseeing skull carved into the cornices. The massive forged-iron chapel gate in the *sacrista baja*, or lower sacristy, separates an exhibition space from a meeting-room. Rainbow glass spills coloured light across the granite walls when the sun breaks through and lights the wide cloisters encircling the open courts.

A monastic simplicity prevails in these courtyards, broken only by the alabaster Gothic arches, carved to resemble lace, or the natural silver flakes in the granite that wink in the light. Highly polished copper pots and kettles placed strategically round the dark palace corridors also reflect broken light. Here, two chairs and a lamp furnish one wall; there, a weathered wooden chest another.

LEFT The Salon Real's carved scallop-shell door leads to the plaza balcony.

OPPOSITE The main salon serves as a lobby for the parador and is furnished with plush velour seating and a collection of antique religious art.

The shift from the severe exterior to the inner salons is as dramatic as the furnishings themselves. The main salon acts as a lobby, in a celebration of red. Bishops' hats and carved saints, gleaming reliquaries and woven tapestries play off the sombre, muted colours of the rich brocades used for the upholstery. This palette of blood-red and olive deflects the eye to the building itself, as if the furnishings were mere ephemera rather than centuries-old, treasured pieces.

Of the parador's 137 guest rooms, the Royal Suite used by the former kings and queens of Spain glories in its wonderful coffered ceilings. Heavily embroidered brocades form a canopy over matching four-poster beds with their highly polished wooden panels and posts. A glassed-in balcony reflects the sort of Moorish influence that is visible all over Spain. In these very private quarters, lengths of gauze curtains protect the occupants from view. With its enchanting historical details, such as closets hidden behind

ABOVE, LEFT AND RIGHT Delicate arches protect the inner arcades of the stone-paved courtyard.

OPPOSITE Sturdy monastic furniture from the parador's past furnishes sheltered seating-areas from the midday sun.

panels of carved wood and a cherished writing-desk, the spacious suite is worthy of its royal heritage.

On a top floor reached by massive stone staircases, the Salon Real, housing an army of blue-velvet-padded wooden chairs as heavy as stone, stands ready for use for formal dinners. A delicate shell – St James's shell, the emblematic scallop of Santiago – is carved above the door to a balcony, from where a private view over the cathedral square, the Plaza do Obradoiro, can be gained. From a distance, the entire edifice of the parador seems to stand in homage to the cathedral itself; bereft of both spire and tower, it reminds us to turn our eye towards the cathedral's Baroque fantasies, which insistently point to Heaven. Yet from this balcony's vantage point, the otherwise severe façade of the parador is dominated by a close-up view of oversized stone fruit, foliage and chains that loom large under the soffit. These classic decorative devices are but a nod in deference to the Baroque celebration that is the city of Santiago de Compostela.

Turning our back to the plaza, we return to the many hushed bedrooms, where gold-voile and heavy-lined print curtains, and shutters, keep the throng out, and quiet prevails. Elaborate embroidery and thick brocade form part of a careful approach to decoration that returns the focus to the inner voyager and to the traveller or pilgrim who, after a long journey, seeks rest and restorative luxury in this city perched on the western edge of Spain's Galician province.

LEFT, TOP AND BOTTOM The curtained gallery in the Royal Suite shields guests from the outside heat while casting a soft shadow of a polychrome wooden sculpture on a mantlepiece.

OPPOSITE Exquisitely carved beds, polished parquet and coffered-wood ceiling panels combine with brocade-and-velour furnishings to create an impression of refined strength in the expansive Royal Suite.

Coastal Comfort
Farmhouse hotel, Getaria

This Basque-Country guest house enjoys a privileged setting on the edge of the Bay of Biscay, near the village of Getaria, and on a clear day the coast of France is visible. Across the Txakoli vineyards, it is possible to see not only the nearby lighthouse, Ratón de Getaria, but also those icons farther up the coast – the lighthouses of Hondarribia and San Sebastián, and of Biarritz in France.

The Hotel Itureggi, although purpose designed and built as a luxury small hotel, successfully masquerades as a Basque farmhouse, its low, sloping chalet roofline with deep overhang being reminiscent of the country houses that line the rural roads of the area. Classic lines and traditional materials conceal a contemporary model of fresh country living. The solid walls built to withstand the blustery weather off the Cantabrian Sea enclose a restful centre of quiet luxury, which offers a charming and soothing welcome reflected in a calm, cool palette of greys and sage-greens.

'My father bought the property fourteen years ago because he liked its location in the middle of nature. He bought it because he loved the site, the views and the vines around the Txakoli area', owner José Ángel

LEFT A railroad-sleeper staircase descends the green hills leading to the main guest house from the family *txoka*.

OPPOSITE The deep-tiled roof overhangs a very sheltered terrace, ideal for convivial outdoor gatherings.

Rodríguez explains. The first part of the restoration began with transforming the existing old family house into a *txoka*, the Basque word for a den or clubhouse, where the clan would gather for winter weekend dinners. This traditional family retreat sits above the new hotel and the remnants of an old stone ruin, where an arched opening of golden stone frames a postcard view of the vineyards as they race up and down the verdant Basque hills to the sea.

The modern adaptation of classic Basque design began with the idea of building a new structure that incorporates the tranquillity of the surroundings into the hotel itself. Rodríguez recalls: 'After repairing the family house, I decided to begin a hotel project. I chose Daniel Rotaeche as designer because of the projects he has done. Together we defined the construction and decor as one. We worked to make the techniques and the detail suit the material, comfort and look.'

More salon than terrace, a sitting-area is sheltered by a multi-paned glass wall that serves to highlight the view as well as to protect guests from the winds off the Bay of Biscay. The deep overhang of the roof shades an outdoor room furnished with cube-shaped, raw-wood tables,

The inviting swimming pool is sheltered from ocean breezes by the ruins of a stone wall, in which an arched doorway provides a stone-framed view of the Bay of Biscay.

wicker furniture, plants and lamps. The classic colonnade, paved with large pebbles set in cement and bordered by quarried stones, shelters an open terrace, from where, after dusk, the lighthouse show can be enjoyed.

Comfort is the key element in the wide, open foyer and lobby living-area. A muted palette of grey, linen and sage is used on the invitingly wide corduroy velour sofas and meticulously painted woodwork. Fat, brightly coloured silk ottomans entice the visitor through a series of stylish sitting-areas. Silk-brocade wing chairs in magenta paisley set off a grouping of zinc ornaments gathered on the side-table near the flat-mantled fireplace. Panels of sawtooth wooden beams frame a wall of soft light, where, by means of silk-gauze drapery, windows and an elaborate nineteenth-century mirror mimic the effect of fog-filtered light.

The sea-mist luminosity that washes through the hotel also brightens the cosy library, with its dark wood and deep-velour furnishings. Calm and order prevail in both design and colour up a wooden staircase with grey-painted banisters and into the bedrooms on the top two floors. Each spacious bedroom, individually designed using different materials and colours, offers a view of sea or mountains. Daniel Rotaeche chose

OPPOSITE Multi-paned glass walls reveal the blue-water vistas and open fields, while protecting the informal seating-areas from weather and wind.

RIGHT, TOP AND BOTTOM Magenta silk paisley wing chairs provide a spot of hot colour in the soft-grey entrance and lobby areas.

sumptuous fabrics by Spanish firm Gaston y Daniela to play off the pristine white bedlinens, contributing a feel of quiet luxury.

The voluminous suite Getaria, named after the nearby home village, is at the top of Itureggi, under the hotel's wide, spreading roof, and has a balcony view of rolling vineyards, fields and sea. Under white-painted exposed beams, a canopied four-poster bed is swathed in olive-grey silk and velour. The colour scheme is mirrored in the creamy marble of the en-suite bathroom. Choice antique tables and chairs complement modern lamps selected for the airiness of their design. The other bedrooms also bear the names of local villages and mountains, such as Orio, Azkizu and Zarautz, and each is given an individuality by means of colours chosen to harmonize with the varied landscapes of the dramatic Basque countryside: the striped earth tones of Zumaia, the white-and-green floral prints of Jaizkibel, and the felted charcoal tones of Zarautz.

Tucked into the shelter of the golden stone ruin, a large swimming pool provides the best views of all, from the wildflower-strewn fields to the distant pale-blue sea. Old outbuildings, grouped against the hillside, now serve the pool area.

As the trend in boutique hotels grows, offering guests an alternative to a private country home, Iturregi provides residents of San Sebastián and Bilbao with a local taste of rural peace, just as it seduces international visitors with its charming Basque-Country hospitality within an exceptional natural environment.

LEFT, TOP AND BOTTOM A substantial wooden staircase and its carved balustrade climb to the first- and second-floor bedrooms, which reflect the cool sea-fog palette in their floors, wall and wood.

OPPOSITE Located on the top floor, the Getaria Suite, named after the charming fishing village near by, has a sea view through two large bull's-eye windows, and boasts a four-poster bed swathed in yards of luxurious silk fabric.

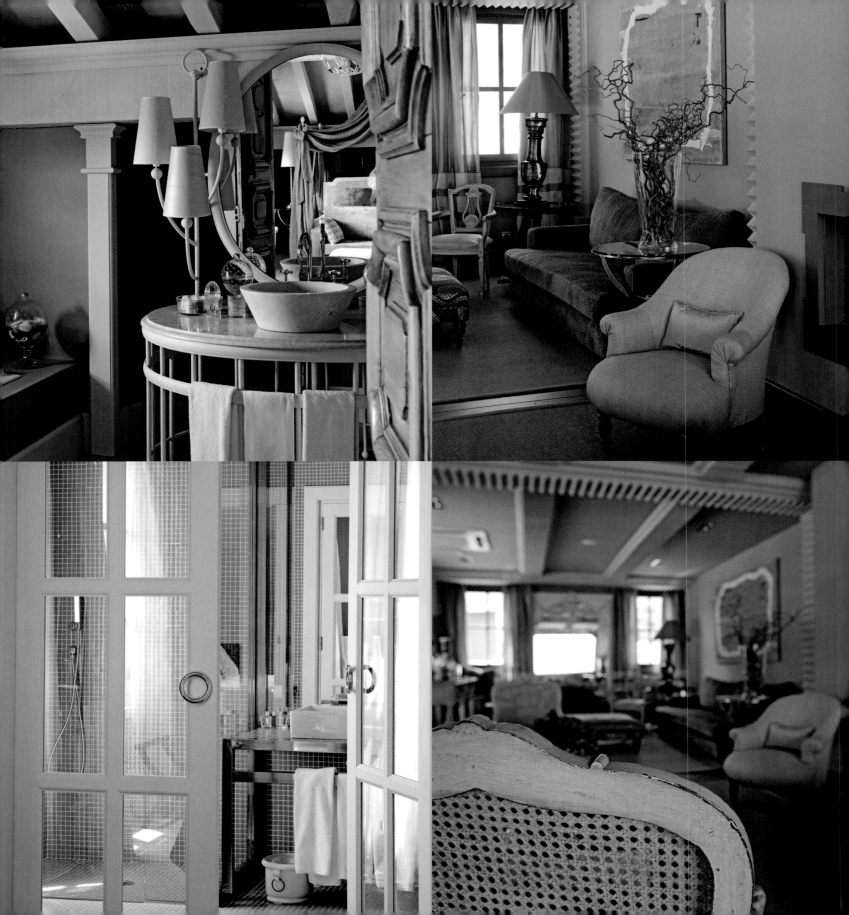

High Drama
Private home, Seville

In the heart of one of Seville's busy residential quarters, the Alfalfa, a crowd gathers over tapas and cold beer around actor Miguel Caiceo – a local boy returning to his Sevillano roots. Fiercely proud of his native city, Caiceo has returned to live in a colourful, art-filled apartment just off the bustling Plaza Alfalfa. In the peaceful, blossom-scented courtyard, once used to stable carriage horses, caged birds now sing and light filters through orange-trees planted in a sunken garden and sheltering the two-storey apartment from the street.

An antiques dealer as well as an actor, Caiceo has created a personal theatre of carefully staged settings: a diverse collection of paintings, together with pieces of antique furniture that serve as little altars to exhibit the numerous historical sculptures and sacred statues. Lions and Christians are everywhere: fierce miniature animals in carved ivory meet polychrome wooden statues salvaged from convents and churches. The colourful entrance leads to a deep, crowded salon humming with personages as diverse as a cobbler in a Sandoval painting and a sixteenth-century wooden sculpture of an anonymous monk. Carmen dances in one

LEFT, TOP AND BOTTOM The enclosed terrace, open to the sky, serves as an outdoor living-area. It is decorated with actor Miguel Caiceo's collection of traditional ceramics and his signature beast – the lion.

painting, a proud toreador poses in porcelain and a pair of bronze *commedia dell'arte* sculptures act as theatrical muses, while across the room a lace-veiled Sevillana poses for Basque painter Francisco Iturrino.

Although Caiceo's art collection dominates, it is the colours of southern Spain, contrasting with the whitewashed exterior walls, that give a sense of geographical location. A particular deep yellow is used as a backdrop to Caiceo's highly personal collection of art and sculpture. Throughout Andalucía, this earthy shade, known as *arena* after the deep-yellow sand of the bullfighting ring, dominates. 'White is for hospitals!' Caiceo proclaims. The same palette of colour runs throughout the apartment: yellow on the walls, a deep leaf-green trim on woodwork and doors, and a muted felt red echoing from a French armchair to an exquisite Persian carpet. Although Caiceo might dismiss the notion of white as a backdrop colour, in fact he uses it effectively as a punctuation mark – as a clean white break between the colour planes of wall and armoire, or to enhance the rich yellow background behind a collection of nineteenth-century porcelain souvenirs of the Grand Tour.

'You could say I am a Sevillano and very proud of it.' Caiceo gestures theatrically around his apartment. 'This is how I feel – Baroque!' Surrounded by the art and objects that he loves, he feels that his home is

With its decor based on a warm palette common to Andalucía, the sitting-room is bathed in deep yellow and trimmed with dark green and bright white. A selection of Caiceo's favourite Spanish paintings hangs on the walls.

an extension of his roots. Nowhere is this more in evidence than in a corner of the living-room, where a carved-wood grape vine wraps sinuously around a wooden pillar and a proud portrait of a real-life Carmen, a tobacco girl, oversees a pair of playful marble lovers and a painted lead figure of the Christ child. The juxtaposition of sacred, and secular elevated by beauty, is a common theme throughout the apartment.

The influence of the Moorish world is present even here, in an urban apartment, where a neat, tiled courtyard affords the interior some morning sun and evening sky. Light floods in and fills the corners of the L-shaped room that is an Ali-Baba's cave of Caiceo's favoured possessions. This light trap, set at the back of the apartment, is an inside garden, with iron furniture brightened with vivid yellow and a wall of antique ceramics and tiles. This is a comfortable sitting-room, as relaxed as the elegant salons are formal. Seventeenth- and eighteenth-century decorative tiles from nearby Triana turn even this unpretentious space into an outside gallery.

The easy-going, chaotic beauty continues in Caiceo's library, where floor-to-ceiling shelves of art books line the room. A beautifully carved side-table displays a seventeenth-century bust of St John and a pair of treasured Meissen vases. A Cuban mahogany secretaire is the diminutive

RIGHT A green, painted balustrade leads to a guest room and a Murillo-inspired copy of the Madonna.

stage for a pair of swirling ceramic dancers by Antonio Peyro and a trio of female torsos on this *altar de mujeres* – a 'tribute to women'.

Parquet floors and a green wooden banister lead upstairs to a sunny guest room presided over by a classic painting of the Madonna and adorned with sixteenth-century silk embroideries and rare leather and parchment books from a monastic collection.

Caiceo's bedroom is the true heart of his home. He reserves some of his favourite and most intimate pieces, a collection of disparate styles and objects, for this room. Each is loved for itself: a magnificent Russian ivory box; a lovely seaside painting by Spanish Impressionist painter Joaquín Sorolla; delicate turquoise jugs from Alcora; a pair of ceramic dogs from Triana; and two Talavera jugs. And while a voluptuous gypsy painted by Córdoba artist Julio Romero de Torres poses above a naughty pair of cupids playing with hearts and fire, a parade from antiquity marches across the pale-grey bookcases that flank a Carlos Vasquez painting over the bed.

While the apartment is a very private retreat from the public, it is far from lonely. In this kingdom of dramatic personages ranging from Hercules to Molière, from the infant Christ to Caiceo's late father, Miguel Caiceo lives as he acts, with passion and humour. In his home neighbourhood of Alfalfa, Caiceo plays host to a cast of thousands who inhabit the colourful rooms of this urban Seville apartment.

Caiceo's bedroom is home to his collection of theatrical books and a number of portraits of such muses as Molière and Shakespeare. A parade of stone and bronze antiquities looks on from above the crowded bookshelves.

OVERLEAF The sunny terrace lights the interior spaces through large picture windows, creating an open feel to this ground-floor Seville apartment.

Visionary Glamour
Restaurant and hotel, Olot

A surfeit of surprises awaits at this inland corner of Catalunya, near the town of Olot. One family's thirteenth-century house has been transformed into a world-class dining-establishment, offering a fresh interpretation of the gastronomy of the Garrotxa region, as well as a completely new experience of destination dining. In this not-so-auspicious location just off the main road to the Pyrenees, simple signage points to a large, solid farmhouse structure that certainly predates the suburban hubbub of petrol stations and nearby shops. This is just the first surprise.

Les Cols is both the family home and the Michelin-starred restaurant of chef Fina Puigdevall. At its stainless-steel professional hearth, she turns a delicate and innovative hand to reinventing the typical dishes of this region, using local produce raised from its mineral-rich volcanic soil. The award-winning restaurant and five stunning new sleeping-pavilions, designed by RCR Arquitectes to reflect the style of Puigdevall's cuisine, are hidden behind the original stone walls of the *masia*.

The façade of the traditional stone *masia*, or Catalan farmhouse, seen from the garden, conceals the avant-garde side of Les Cols's architecture and design.

Col means 'cabbage' in Catalan, and at the entrance to the masia is an unpretentious cabbage patch; guests are invited to follow the rusty-patinated steel path towards the shelter of the old stone and brick. Once within the old walls, the focus is entirely on the internal landscape of courtyard, barnyard and kitchen – and the new, other-worldly sleeping-pavilions. The path to the restaurant leads past the kitchen, over a shallow, flat pond – a slice of water layered over polished black pebbles, hinting at the volcanic foundation that underpins the soil here in the Garrotxa.

In the dining-room, we see the beginning of a dialogue between steel and glass: steel walls, with a burnt-crust texture, complement rolling chairs made from solid-steel sheets burnished to a deep metallic-gold finish; a wall of glass lights an alcove of golden steel dining-tables and -chairs. The play of disparate surfaces whets the appetite for more. In a bold visual and experiential move, an extraordinary steel dining-table, which seats forty, extends through the heart of the building. At either end of this shimmering cavern of gold and light, windows give on to a raised barnyard complete with strutting chickens, a vegetable garden and an inviting manicured lawn sheltered by old stone walls.

LEFT, TOP AND BOTTOM Custom-built folded steel dining-tables and -chairs float in one lava-coloured room of the restaurant, while bare steel ribbons enclose the glass entrance.

OPPOSITE Water, glass, steel and volcanic stone define the textures of the five sleeping-pavilions.

Transitions from rustic stone and traditional Catalan architecture to a futuristic vision of glass and steel continually surprise, as at the entrance to the newly constructed sleeping-pavilions. Ivy-clad walls of dark-grey stucco conceal a simple, solitary entrance hall that leads to the Pavilion's five extraordinary glass sleeping-rooms. Underscored by a tall, bare, steel table the colour of burnt earth, the lava gravel floor reminds one that La Garrotxa is a land formed by fire and time, with Olot being on the very doorstep of the Volcano national park. A simple sliding band of steel separates guests from the outside world; within, a maze of steel tubes directs guests to an elevated stainless-steel walkway leading to the glass boxes, which float over a frozen flow of manmade material, designed to look like volcanic lava.

Cabbage-green glass panels swivel on steel pins to break the apparently solid corridor that leads to the rooms. Blasted opaque to provide privacy, they form a crystalline hedge bordering the shiny gangplank that leads to the unnumbered pavilion doors. Designed by three young Catalan architects, these five elegantly monastic rooms embrace the literal and metaphorical need to rest and to digest the food that feeds the spirit as well as the body.

OPPOSITE A single common table, built of bronze-coloured steel and capable of seating forty, runs the length of the central room in the restaurant and all the way to the two glass doors that lead to the garden.

RIGHT, TOP AND BOTTOM The narrow entrances that lead to the pavilions provide minimalist thresholds to the stark glass rooms beyond.

Each pavilion has its own private courtyard, paved in volcanic rock, a texture that also extends beneath the glass floors of the pavilions themselves. While one may at first find it disorientating to stand on apparently floating glass, the courtyard lava gardens anchor the open sky, visible through the glass walls and roof. The lone piece of furniture in each pavilion is puzzled together from cabbage-blue metallic-leather ottomans or cushions, which for the night are dressed with black sheets to form a double bed. Starlight and moonlight filter through the glass ceilings to lighten dark dreams, though at the touch of a button, flat black panels descend to shield the skylight over the bed and shut out the moon and stars from these ethereal private worlds.

The bathroom gives a clear contemporary nod to classic Japanese *ryokan* soaking tubs. The warm-water tub, measuring 1.2 metres (4 feet) deep, is kept continually running and always full, while a rainforest showerhead sprays water on to the same black polished stones as are found in the kitchen pool. To soak under the star-studded night sky is a lesson in quietude and space.

This extreme Spanish design could perhaps exist only as a reaction to such a primitive and old place. In contrast to the conventional nature of the rest of Olot, Les Cols pulls the visitor in two diverse directions — to the thirteenth-century façade of the original farmhouse, and to the futuristic gleam of its stunning glass sleeping-pavilions.

OPPOSITE A square reflecting pool mirrors the spare stainless-steel workstation of the restaurant kitchen.

RIGHT, TOP AND BOTTOM A hedge of steel poles and a lava-cinder path lead to the sleeping-pavilions via an elegant stainless-steel walkway framed by glass privacy panels.

New Vintage Baroque
Wine complex and hotel, La Rioja

The vast landscapes of the Rioja region, the open plains bordered by the Ebro River and shielded by the Cantabrian Mountains, are famed for their vineyards. La Rioja Alavesa, its name — from Alava — harking back to its Arabic past, is one of the three main wine zones, producing deep-red wines. After a long, contested history, it is looking to a prosperous and peaceful future, marked by one of Spain's major contemporary design milestones: Frank O. Gehry's design for the Marqués de Riscal's new City of Wine. Gehry seems to dream in three dimensions, and his design for the wine centre is the realization of a vision that unites the original nineteenth-century winery, a modern luxury hotel and a trendy 'vinotherapy' spa on the edge of the once-sleepy village of Elciego.

On a winter's day, bare vines march towards the buildings, as if beckoned by a cluster of ebullient streams of colour — banners that proclaim Gehry's innovative use of titanium and stainless steel. Flying like a three-dimensional coat of arms, this frozen metallic wave echoes the colours of the Marqués de Riscal: red for the wine, gold for the mesh on the Riscal bottles and silver for the bottle capsule. The swirling, thin titanium and steel sheets hang effortlessly from a steel framework that is rooted deep into the historic foundations of the original wine cellar — dubbed the 'Cathedral' — thereby merging the nineteenth and twenty-first centuries.

LEFT, TOP AND BOTTOM Pink-tinted titanium curves over a visible support of metal rafters and beams, to frame the historic vineyards of the Marqués de Riscal winery.

OPPOSITE Frank Gehry's hotel structure for the City of Wine, made of local sandstone topped with a tricoloured wave of pink-and-gold titanium and mirror-finished stainless steel, seems to suspend motion beneath the changing skies of La Rioja Alavesa.

This emphatically modern wine complex houses a hotel, a spa for 'wine therapy', an exclusive restaurant, a meeting and conference centre and a banquet hall, all built over the original underground nineteenth-century 'Cathedral' wine cellar. Beneath the vines' roots, Gehry has also built a new foundation and cellar, adjacent to the old and plunging deep into the bedrock of Rioja. Above the surrounding vine-covered landscape, and supported on three pillars the foundations of which reach deep into the new cellars, blocks of local sandstone lift the undulating roofline, which frames with a Baroque flourish the view of the medieval village church of San Andrés. Reflecting sky, clouds, sun and rain, the metal ribbons contrast with the matt surfaces of the sandstone walls and the bare dirt fields between the rows of vines. The dramatic billowing canopy that defines the exterior also provides an elegant transition to the stark, modern interior that opens out in the welcoming reception area.

For the interior, Gehry chose Spanish interior architect and designer Javier Muñoz as his collaborator. Together they play with strong colour throughout the interiors of the hotel: from deep burgundy to fire-engine red, from orange to gold to ochre; white stands out against the earthy colours of raw woods and leather. Textures are smooth and matt, from the wooden floor parquet to leather and raw-maple plywood panelling. In a suave game of passing design elements back and forth, Gehry designed the stainless-steel lamps hanging from the bar while Muñoz designed the tables and chairs. Red-felted Pop chairs, thick wool carpets and soft sandstone contrast with shiny copper panels and acres of glass in the spacious reception area that links the wine bar and terraces; natural tones of leather, wood and paper create soft cocoons in the private guest rooms.

RIGHT, TOP Gehry designed many of the interior details, including a customized wine store and copper-sheathed service counter for the Gastronomic Restaurant.

RIGHT, BOTTOM An arrangement of red, white and blue in the hotel lobby includes a new lamp system called *Clouds*, designed by Gehry and inspired by Noguchi paper lanterns.

The rooms and suites are a showcase of late twentieth- and early twenty-first-century international design, with Gehry designing many of the furnishings himself, such as the ethereal puffs of *Cloud* lamps, and the undulating leather headboards. Each room boasts archival design items that fit together smoothly — a low Eero Saarinen table here, a floating Gehry lamp there, tables and chairs by Modernist icon Alvar Aalto. And always the designers play with materials, from 2.5-cm-thick (1 in.) maple plywood, the exposed edges of which provide a decorative touch, to paper-like lamps, made of a polyester fleece that has been treated several times and looks and feels like strong, slightly fibrous paper, inspired by Japanese-American designer Isamu Noguchi.

The main hotel building contains the two restaurants, both of which are served from the distinguished kitchen of Francis Paniego, and feature a mix of traditional recipes from the chef's mother and his own avant-garde dishes. As elsewhere in the hotel, the building is decoration enough in itself, with large wood-framed windows that slope inward to reveal the structural design underpinning the lyrical roof. Seated on iconic bright-orange Panton chairs and surrounded by Gehry's pencil-sketch design both on the walls and underfoot in a customized carpet, diners relax in the casual, sunlit ambience of Restaurant 1860. Red dominates the Gastronomic Restaurant, from the fabric wall and carpet to exquisite red Baccarat water glasses. A series of painted discs by contemporary artist Fernando Bermejo floats alongside Gehry's stainless-steel suspension lamps, while an onyx-and-copper service bar protects the Gehry-designed glass wine cellar.

OPPOSITE The Gehry Suite and its private terrace overlook the Baroque church of San Andrés in Elciego. Natural finishes of pale wood parquet, earthen-coloured leather upholstery and stark white plaster walls complement the well-chosen contemporary and classic mid-twentieth-century furniture.

RIGHT, TOP AND BOTTOM Gehry's *Cloud* lamps and undulating leather headboards are the signature of his eponymous suite in the main hotel building.

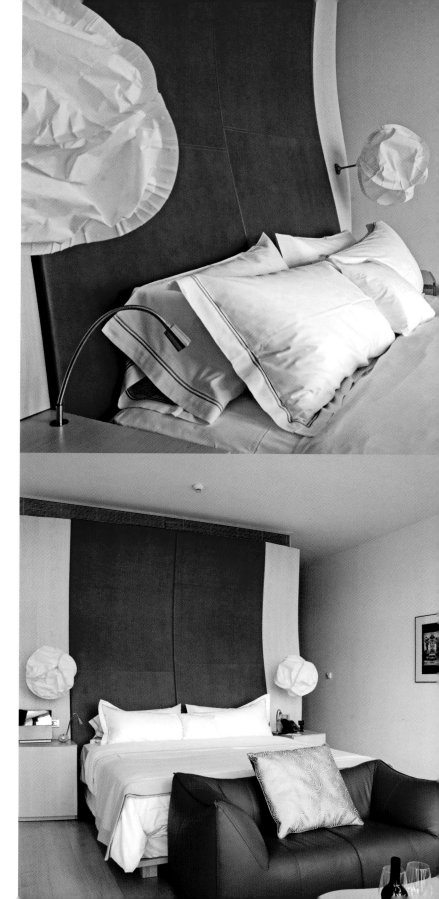

The lower level of the hotel's separate annex houses the City of Wine's Caudalie Vinothérapie Spa, which is devoted to wine- and grape-based treatments. Here again, Javier Muñoz boldly defines with colour and material. Wine-red walls and a frieze of twisting vine roots play off a light-sandstone wall and dark-slate floors and pools. Red-leather loungers seem to stretch into infinity in the calm and sober atmosphere dictated by Muñoz's order and repetition. The red-on-red treatment, recalling strong colours used in the south, fittingly keeps the idea of wine in the forefront.

From the wine bar off the lobby to the top floor, which houses a cosy lounge/library with an open fire, Gehry integrates interior design with the architecture. Nestled into floating ribbons of steel, the lounge perches like an eagle's eyrie, with a panoramic view across the Rioja plain. Like the wine bar's wall of bottle niches, the floor-to-ceiling bookshelves define the function of the room while imposing a sense of order on the thousand volumes at hand. Italian-leather chairs and tables face a copper-fronted fireplace that echoes the thin metal tile of the roofs.

Aside from its standing as one of the world's most architecturally distinguished wineries and hotels, the Marqués de Riscal's City of Wine is founded on one of Spain's deepest cellars and celebrates a legacy of wine-making. The original cellar building houses a priceless collection of vintage wines, so, while modern wine-making facilities take this Rioja classic into the future, the cool stone tunnels cradle untouched barrels and bottles from the past. The historic tasting-room sits above these moss-lined cellars and, with a nod to the stone construction of the winery's past, invites visitors to discover the vintage classics now housed under one extraordinary roof — the soaring roof that Frank Gehry built.

Seen from a distant winter vineyard, the Marqués de Riscal's City of Wine mirrors the ever-changing sky of La Rioja Alavesa, and seems to support the historic Baroque tower of San Andrés Church.

Rural Elegance
Country hotel, La Coruna

In the Miño area of Galicia in western Spain, farm and wilderness meet at Casa Grande Fontao, a seventeenth-century Galician finca transformed by its passionate owner into a most elegant *casa rural* that sleeps fourteen guests in seven simple en-suite bedrooms.

Owner Mari Freire has a deep attachment to this special place. Her father was born in this house, one of ten children working the finca at the turn of the nineteenth century. At first glance, the simple air of another time seems to filter out the modern world, kept from intruding by the untouched exterior stucco and stone walls. Ferns and brambles soften the rough stone walls and paths — that underlying granite surface that marks the dark, damp mood of Galicia — and lend the house an air of 'Sleeping Beauty in the woods'. Weathered doors and shutters create a semblance of an old family home abandoned, its edges darkened by time.

But Mari Freire has struck a note that perfectly balances a gentle nostalgia for the past with an elegant sense of the present. Together with

LEFT, TOP Centuries of stucco soften the austere traditional façade of Mari Freire's family home, now converted to an elegant guest house.

LEFT, BOTTOM Rough stone framing around windows and doors is typical of farmhouse construction in Galicia.

OPPOSITE The windowed *galeria* overhangs and shelters the large picture window of the main-floor salon.

local architect José Mantiñan, she has created a deceptively simple showcase of rustic comfort in this welcoming *casa rural*.

Hefty slabs of local granite pave the entry into the ground-floor living-spaces, uniting kitchen, dining-room and spacious salon. Although the materials used to renew the house are the same simple traditional elements of stucco, whitewash, stone and wood that are found throughout Galicia, they are artfully joined with contemporary materials and well-chosen restored antique furniture.

The informal dining-area, with its original stone sink beneath a shuttered window, once served as the house's main kitchen. Now a service kitchen fills the original *bodega*, or wine cellar, where a spring-water-driven dynamo once turned to create electricity for twelve bare lightbulbs – a luxury in the kind of rural living now recalled here by the presence of a plain galvanized bucket and water-jug. When such simple elements decorate the interiors, the eye turns easily to the green view from every red-shuttered window that frames an unspoilt picture of stone walls enclosing nature's spring glory.

The main sitting-room boasts a large, unobstructed window, which overlooks a garden with granite steps and the remains of a typical *horreo*,

One large garden window dominates the main salon, revealing the stone, beamed construction in a fresh contemporary light.

or freestanding granary, particular to Galicia. Large hooks once used to hold doors open remain as a reminder of the finca's agricultural past. Now, the owner uses glass vases to reflect light from the glazed opening farther into the shadowed recesses of the house. These exterior and interior exchanges of light and scenery are as important on sunny spring days as on those days of grey and overcast skies for which Galicia is notorious.

The upper floor of Casa Grande Fontao soars right up to the exposed roof, showing the beautiful curving bare beams of what was the old hayloft. In a modern solution to comfort and design, the ceiling of the salon is panelled with exposed natural-fibre insulation material, creating a look at once elegant and rustic and matching the exposed-stone walls and raw-wood floors. Freire has placed a cherished family heirloom – a marquetry chair belonging to her mother – next to a stately bookcase filled with original editions and other treasures. Most of the polished furniture, built of local cherrywood and chestnut, comes from nearby Asturias, and, with its simple rustic warmth, unites the separate salons.

Under the eaves, a quiet bedroom sports pristine white like a banner of civilization: fine linens ironed to old-fashioned standards dress a simple

OPPOSITE The original kitchen, with thick stone walls and shuttered windows, now harbours a sunny breakfast area.

RIGHT, TOP AND BOTTOM Deep windowsills as thick as the stone walls offer impromptu shelving space for a lovely stoneware basket and a rudimentary sink with a casual 'bar service' in a galvanized tub.

bed with a local chestnut headboard; a pair of delicate French armchairs is covered in pale-cream linen. Each bedroom shares the same spare palette of natural-wood floors, exposed beams and oxblood-red shutters, but enjoys a different view of the open space surrounding the house and reflects a different quality of light.

A separate, small farm building, now housing a private suite, faces a eucalyptus vale that scents the morning breeze. A slice of silver light streams into the room through a narrow, shuttered window, lighting the bare necessities of desk, rocking-chair and night-table — all that is needed to enjoy the country lifestyle.

Galerias, or glassed-in balconies, feature in much of Galician architecture in cities and towns, and are evident here at rural Casa Grande Fontao as well. An oxblood-red balcony juts out from the east wall and captures the winter and morning light, diffusing it into the elevated salon, the former hayloft. Here, as in all the open public spaces, there is an inherent invitation to sit and study the view from the wall of windows.

OPPOSITE The wood-and-glass *galeria* perches over the garden walls and faces the morning light.

BELOW, LEFT An unadorned, elegant staircase and traditional table combine to create an effect of simple grace in the entrance to the separate bedroom wing.

BELOW, RIGHT Thick interior stone walls are dressed in layers of clean white stucco, creating a softly framed doorway into the main salon.

Throughout the house, Mari Freire has displayed her collection of local contemporary artists' paintings. Both Javier Correa Corredoira's and Alberto Franco's paintings remind us that we are firmly planted in this century, with their playful combination of strong colour and contemporary graphic images. The fusion of these personal and historical perspectives, both central to Freire's affections, is the vital element that elevates a romantic pile of stones to an outstanding example of a country home.

Rustic charm and minimalist arrangements of finely finished old furniture balance each other perfectly in the uncontrived setting of Casa Grande Fontao, while the serene hand of Mari Freire smoothes a blanket of calm across comfortable interiors that match the secluded Galician location of the house.

OPPOSITE Dressed in fine white linen, a large double bed made of simple rustic wood furnishes this spare but luxurious bedroom.

ABOVE Another guest room, lit by a quartet of shuttered windows that filter the soft Galician light, creates an oasis of calm repose in a dramatic landscape.

Hidden Splendour

Historic town house, Cadíz

Cadíz wraps its fortressed arms around an ancient port that has whispered of the comings and goings of ships ever since the Phoenicians founded this merchant city in about 1100 BC. Built on a spit of sand jutting out into the Bay of Cadíz, the old city, or *casco antiguo*, has been protected for thirteen centuries from tides, pirates and politics. With its romantic profile of stone walls, Baroque churches and countless private towers, Cadíz is visible from far out at sea. The soaring lookout towers, *las torres mirador*, were built atop the houses of prominent, fiercely competitive merchants, enabling them to view, and plan their trade with, incoming ships even before these dropped anchor in the harbour.

Within the old city walls, wooden balconies overhang a warren of pedestrian streets, harking back to Arab times, as does much of the architecture of Andalucía. In one street, a suggestion of later glory – of the prosperous eighteenth century – hides behind a pair of massive mahogany doors, heritage of the trade with the Americas. Crowned by delicate floral and figurative plasterwork, the doors pivot open to reveal a courtyard wider and more elegant than the street itself. This is a most graceful invitation to enter into the Cadíz house known as La Bella Escondida – the 'hidden beauty'.

Precise and rational design dominated the city's architecture in its golden era of trade and wealth. Three hundred years later, Manuel Morales

LEFT, TOP The ornately carved Moorish door of the Cadíz town house called La Bella Escondida opens into the first-floor living-quarters.

LEFT, BOTTOM The ground-floor courtyard, paved with a chequerboard of marble surrounded by terracotta tiles, serves as a buffer against a busy shopping street.

OPPOSITE The street-side façade of La Bella Escondida features iron-balustrade balconies and ornately carved plasterwork above a mahogany entrance door.

de Jódar, Sevillano interior designer, has breathed life once again into the beautiful stately home, or *casa palacio*, that lies behind the classic eighteenth-century façade. In plain view, yet hidden, in the centre of Cadíz's chic shopping district, La Bella Escondida contains in its name a cryptic reference to its past. Although the house soars eight levels above the street, its exquisitely tiled octagonal tower, part of its 'hidden beauty', remains invisible from ground level; and a romantic legend associated with an earlier owner provides another clue to the name.

'The owner's beloved youngest daughter took vows of silence and entered a convent', Morales explains. 'Saddened at his loss, he built the most beautiful tower in Cadíz, high enough to see down into the cloister where she walked every evening. From the top of the fourth floor he could still see his "hidden beauty".'

One might say that today it is the house itself that has been revealed by Morales's deft hand with colours and textiles, and his passionate regard for his region's history. 'Originally sailing from Genoa, boats flew between Cadíz and the continents. Everything from the Americas — wood, spices, coffee, silver, tobacco. This house remembers that.' The elaborate interiors of this designer's house reflect its international heritage, which is deeply rooted in local history.

OPPOSITE A glazed, wooden gallery, which has been painted a soft sea-blue, connects every room of the first-floor living-quarters and floods the interior with southern light.

RIGHT The exquisite tiled-and-painted tower of this former merchant's house is one of many still standing in the old town of Cadíz. During the golden age of exploration, it allowed for communication between the merchant and his ships before they entered port.

OVERLEAF The main salon, lit by three Murano glass chandeliers, is a wonderful showcase for Morales's porcelain sculptures, lamps and frames of coral branches and seashells.

Leaving the noise of the street behind and passing through a sombre vestibule, guests enter a sun-drenched courtyard, now glass-roofed on the fourth-floor level. Morales opened up this interior courtyard, styled like a miniature public plaza, with elegant and rational proportions, soaring arched windows and openings of bull's-eye glass. It functions as an intermediate public space, giving access to mezzanine offices and wrought-iron interior balconies that look over a chequered marble floor and carved stone pillars; coral-coloured niches house carved stone fruit in marble vases beside their twin *trompe l'œil* frescoes. The transition to the living-quarters above, via a matching pair of Imperial-style staircases, accentuates the formal approach. The stone stairwell is a fitting overture, forming a private gallery of historical prints and local paintings of Cadíz.

This second entrance to La Bella Escondida leads to Morales's private living-spaces, where a wood-and-glass interior gallery acts as an airy foyer connecting all the first-floor rooms. The colour of the gallery, a particular blue typical of Cadíz, echoes the sea, the sky and a pale silk ribbon on a portrait of a great-grandmother, one of many paintings, depicting family and local personages, that welcome guests.

The main salon faces the street, and incorporates a glassed-in exterior balcony that overlooks the busy evening promenade. Moorish-influenced *galerias* shutter the long, narrow room, also shielded from the strong summer sun by heavy curtains in green, red and yellow, hung from eight gold-leafed box valances from a Valencian palace. Morales has lit the salon with a stunning trio of Venetian chandeliers that hang against a green

LEFT, TOP Gold-and-white frames and fixtures in the dining-room stand out against the pale-blue plaster walls.

LEFT, BOTTOM A rare collection of mercury-glass vases, candlesticks and figurines brightens an otherwise sombre corner of a sitting-room.

OPPOSITE Dressed in white-and-gold Italian porcelain, the formal dining-room is a luxurious haven dedicated to entertaining.

ceiling with aubergine-coloured beams. A band of Neo-classical nineteenth-century tiles, also from Valencia, anchors soft-red and pea-green painted walls. The use of these strong colours in darkened rooms, contrasting with the whitewashed, sun-bleached city outside, creates a haven of calm and luxury just a few steps above the busy streets.

Like the early merchant-ship owners, Morales, a passionate collector, often reaches across the Mediterranean as well as the Atlantic to furnish his showcase home. Solid eighteenth-century velour English club chairs balance a delicate Majorcan armchair upholstered in traditional island fabric. Two striking full-length portraits in black balance the dark piano, a secular altar adorned with a model ship, a fitting reminder of Cadíz's past. Collections of mercury-glass (silvered-glass) vases and statues of the Virgin Mary, Chinese figurines, English clocks and French floral panels fill the rooms and entice the visitor to inspect them more closely.

Most striking are the Baroque white-shell-and-coral mirror frames that book-end the long salon and breakfast-room. They are from a new collection of porcelain frames, chandeliers and obelisks of pristine white shells and red coral branches, a collaboration between Morales and the Italian porcelain-design house of Rita Dal Prà. Morales declares imperiously, 'To be Spanish is to be Baroque!' and he embraces this maxim in his own design work.

Although the previous night's dinner party might have ended in classic Spanish fashion at 5 a.m., in the dining-room the table is nonetheless dressed in impeccable white linen and set with a collection of gold-trimmed white Estes porcelain initialled 'M.M.', evidence of the owner's love of entertaining. Flawlessly painted walls are finished with perfect and lively colour; this time a pure, deep blue, together with white highlights

LEFT, TOP Hammered-metal wall sconces illuminate a mantlepiece and a collection of portraits, including one unusually hung within a mirror.

LEFT, BOTTOM A collection of seashell- and coral-inspired ceramic obelisks, designed by Morales, graces the living-room sideboard.

and polished dark wood, creates a harmonious backdrop for a collection of gold-framed classical oil paintings. The eye is drawn to the painted ceiling, with its seventeenth-century flower-strewn Murano chandelier. Two beautiful bull's-eye lights hover above deep-raspberry brocades that frame the open doors leading to the central glass gallery, the elegant aubergine 'butler's pantry' and the practical kitchen.

Although Morales and his partner often entertain visiting friends from Seville and Madrid, they also have their own quiet haven in the private rooms that open off the square gallery. A small sitting-room is awash with bronze-filtered light and filled with the obligatory homage to the corrida – a pair of toreadors framed in red and white, flanking a mirrored portrait.

From this cosy retreat, magnificent, carved mahogany double doors open on to the master bedroom, where a bed worthy of royalty waits to inspire dreams. It was, in fact, this bed that began the affair with the house. Morales was led to Cadíz to look at a stunning Empire-style bed that, legend has it, was once given as a gift to a lover by Francis, Duke of Cadíz and King Consort of Spain. Not only did the designer recognize the value of the inlaid marquetry and decorative bronze fittings and buy the bed, but he also fell in love with the the house itself and the many legends attached to it. Restored from courtyard to tower, La Bella Escondida is no longer hidden: its once-cloistered beauty now shines for all to see.

LEFT, TOP A rosary made of amber and carnelian – a family heirloom – rests on the custom-made, watered-silk bedclothes.

LEFT, BOTTOM In a whimsical reference to the Battle of Trafalgar, the master bathroom has been furnished with Empire-era furniture and details, while its walls have been painted to resemble battle-tent drapery.

OPPOSITE Hung with rich silk brocade and with gold detailing on the walls, the master bedroom is dominated by a magnificent Empire bed, decorated with delicate bronze-and-ebony marquetry.

Catalan Spirit
Art studio, Cap Creus

Two starkly different structures owned by the Catalan artist Moisés Tibau grace an olive-grove whose 618 trees sway like a silver-green ocean. These trees, the modern studio and the restored *cabaña* overlook the blue Mediterranean Sea far off Cap Creus at the north end of the Costa Brava. The buildings are set into the landscape of the natural Cap Creus flora: rosemary that blooms in January, cacti with chartreuse flowers, agave, and century plants; bougainvillea drapes across doorways. Created by legions of early settlers – Phoenicians, Greeks and Romans – miles of stone terraces have been maintained for centuries by olive-growers and landowners in order to keep out destructive wild boar truffling for snails or sharpening a tusk against the flinty stone. In spring, the heady scent of olive-blossom mingles sweetly with the salty sea air.

The first small structure – the *cabaña* – was originally built as an agricultural refuge from the fierce *tramuntana* wind and used by workers during the pruning and harvesting of the olive-trees or when tending the dry-stone terraces. Now Tibau, a native of Cadaqués, hosts weekend gatherings of family and friends here, while function still dictates the simple decor: a wooden water-keg hangs from a curtain rod; a mobile of assorted iron pots and pans swings from the blue-painted beams. The

LEFT, TOP Hidden behind a screen of swirling olive-trees, the painting studio of Catalan artist Moisés Tibau is a safe retreat in the strong Mediterranean wind.

LEFT, BOTTOM A minimal slate-and-stone altar sits surrounded by cacti, umbrella pines and olive-trees on a slate-flagged terrace.

OPPOSITE Built of traditional materials, the painting studio climbs the dry-stone terraces that define the topographical curves of rugged Cap Creus.

traditional plaster corner fireplace comes into use in the winter; the kitchen is otherwise simply furnished with a wooden table and an assortment of reed chairs. Water-jugs, gourds and the bare necessities to make an impromptu meal conjure an air of an earlier time, but in fact are just as contemporary in Tibau's world. Neither electricity nor plumbing impinge in this simple *cabaña*, leaving it just as it was a hundred years ago.

Placed against the pink stucco wall and sheltered from most of the prevailing winds, an iron table crafted by Tibau serves as a focus for dining and conversation. It is here that *alioli* is pounded in the traditional olive-wood mortar until thick enough to hold the pestle in its garlicky emulsion. A fire of olive-branches heats the stone walls of the historic terraces, and grills the fresh fish that Tibau brings in from his boat at nearby Portlligat. Wire and iron bars support a reed awning in summer, while in winter the sun filters on to the sheltered terrace.

A walk up through the olive-grove leads to the painting studio built by Tibau, where he turns his back on the view of the sea, including the distant glimpse of *el far del mundo*, the 'lighthouse at the end of the world' – the first place on the Iberian peninsula that is touched by the sun. The studio, constructed at the top of this well-tended olive-grove like a solid ship turned into the wind, serves as a place for creating paintings and ceramics, and as a showroom. Made of materials and with techniques that are used

OPPOSITE A simple shelter built of stones from the terrace, and once used to house tools, now acts as a focal point for the outside terrace.

RIGHT, TOP The interior of the *cabaña*, where impromptu meals are cooked on a variety of grills and steel pans hung, like a modern sculpture, above traditional Catalan furniture.

RIGHT, BOTTOM An abandoned farm tool and well-used grill decoratively stud the stone wall of the old tool shed.

in every Catalan fishing village, the spacious two-level studio has terracotta brick walls, concrete rafters and the signature Catalan vaulting for the tiled, limewashed ceiling. A glass wall faces north towards the French border and Perpignan, flooding the room with generous light.

While a bed and minimal kitchen make the studio an inviting guest room for the overspill of visitors to the Tibau family home in Cadaqués in summer, this artist and fisherman normally reserves the space for his private use as a retreat and place of work. The studio walls are plastered in white stucco, which also flows on to large canvases serving as floating backgrounds for an anthology of oversized chilli peppers, sprouting seeds and ancient urns. Tibau draws from his native setting of sea and stone for his square canvases; painted with earth pigments, sea life swims on coloured canvases that appear as salty as the sea just hundreds of metres from the studio door.

The simple rectangular footprint of the floor is divided at an angle by steps leading from the showroom to the studio space, office and kitchen. Stepping up to the studio from the gallery, two workbenches culled from a garage and a farm are littered with feathers, bones and seeds, natural elements that inspire Tibau's work. A series of large open platters glazed and fired at nearby ceramics centre La Bisbal adorns a studio table once

LEFT, TOP AND BOTTOM Tibau finds his inspiration in natural materials, such as a string of chilli peppers and a table-top arrangment of fishbones, dried grapes and woven reed baskets.

OPPOSITE A pair of painted oversized vases and platters is displayed on a customized iron table in front of a trio of Tibau's large canvases in the square-windowed 'showroom' of the artist's studio.

used by local fishermen and left propped against Salvador Dalí's iconic house just outside Cadaqués. The economy of the materials used by Tibau – a fishbone, a branch of coral, or a plate of squid and rice – contrasts agreeably with the grandeur of the open spaces and the history of artists, including Dalí, Picasso and Duchamp, who left their mark on Cap Creus.

A built-in cistern catches seasonal rainwater to serve the simple bathroom, which functions with found materials: a tiny marble basin, raw brick walls, a solitary copper-pipe spout. In the kitchen area, tile strips form a mosaic splashback and functional brass hardware complements the glazed terracotta sink, near which is a tower of handmade fishing-baskets, salvaged from the bin by Tibau and preserved for their intricate beauty.

The large metal-framed windows of the sturdy atelier look out on the flurry of olive-leaves agitated by the afternoon wind – one of those folkloric winds that blow madness as well as dust into every crevice of the brain. And while the studio and the *cabaña* give flight to the artist's imagination, they are well grounded in this wild, arid landscape with its agave, rosemary, lavender and *immortelles*. This last variety is a plant found in every Catalan house, from fishermen's huts to grand homes; its dry, pale-straw flowers are used to scent windows and fireplaces in summer, as well as to ward off mosquitoes. Umbrella pines litter the ancient terraces with pine cones, while a carpet of dry needles softens the harsh, rocky landscape that informs Moisés Tibau's work and harbours his studio retreat.

OPPOSITE Olive-trees, pines and bougainvillea camouflage the north side of the studio and help shade an open concrete terrace.

RIGHT, TOP Olive-oil and wine flasks above the window reflect light that also bounces off a tile-vaulted ceiling.

RIGHT, BOTTOM The remains of a Roman amphora, cradled as carefully as a work of art.

Scale and Substance

Art museum, San Sebastian

'I'm of the opinion, and this is very important to me, that we are from somewhere. Ideally, we are from one place, where our roots are, but we should reach out to the entire world and borrow ideas from other cultures. Any place can be perfect for the person who's adapted to it. Here in the Basque Country I feel like I'm where I belong, like a tree adapted to the land, but with branches that reach out to the rest of the world. I'm trying to create the work of a person, my own work because I am who I am, and since this is where I'm from, my work will take on particular tones, a sort of dark light, our light.' Eduardo Chillida

There are perhaps no more eloquent words about the work of the late Eduardo Chillida than his own evocative description. And, narrowing the focus, those same words could be seen as describing the very farmhouse/studio/museum that he created to house his life's works: a place that once went by the name of the Zabalaga Farmhouse, and is now known to the whole world as Chillida-Leku, or Chillida's Place.

The historic Basque Zabalaga Farmhouse, once used as the working studio of Eduardo Chillida, now houses the permanent collection of the Chillida-Leku museum near San Sebastian.

A long, slow walk takes the visitor up a gentle slope of parkland, studded with monumental steel artworks like a giant child's game of building blocks. These are the signature sculptures for which this Basque artist is best known. And while Chillida conceived the entire museum as a dynamic artwork itself, with pieces going out to and returning from international exhibitions, the heart of his magnum opus is housed in the large stone-and-timber Basque farmhouse. This five-hundred-year-old granite-and-wood building, which once served as both barn and house, was initially reborn as Chillida's studio — as detailed in a painting by his son Pedro that hangs in the private family house. Together with architect Joaquín Montero, Chillida restored the farmhouse and barn so that they seem like sculptures themselves.

A wonderful *Alice in Wonderland* feeling permeates the farmhouse/studio, which initially looms large and brooding, surrounded by a pad of cut-granite cobblestones. The 'dark light', that special Basque light to which Chillida refers, pours in through an oversized glass door flanked by moss-covered stone buttresses. A large skylight drops more light on to a pale, sand-coloured polished cement floor that stretches into a space

Stone, steel and wood are the recurring materials Chillida used in his sculpture and in creating his studio/museum.

resembling a vast playing-field, on which dozens of sculptures are displayed. It is when standing in the midst of this huge open space, its towering roof supported by giant tree-trunk beams, that we seem to shrink to Alice-like proportions.

Chillida used cut oak-tree columns and beams to support and brace the roof and walls, giving an effect of branches that, in his own words, 'reach out to the rest of the world'. Spliced, stepped and pegged, the oaks become sculptures in themselves, perching elegantly on stone pedestals. Decorative as well as structural, the beams are as oversized as the building itself, their raw finish, open grain and water stains evincing a special sort of attention to detail matched by a granite-trimmed window frame or a cut-stone arch.

Among these vast timbers, pegs and wedges as large as mallets seem to shrink. A massive beam sets off a stair railing. The studio dwarfs the outside sculptures, redefining the visitor's sense of scale; the play of volume and negative space here invites a more intimate understanding of Chillida's artistic experiments with the monumental, which include hollowing out a once-solid mountain, Mount Tindaya, to create a human-scale space within its vastness. Similarly, moving through the studio we are finally brought to an understanding of the empty space in every sculpture by Chillida – a place to be at home within the greater context of nature.

A wall-sized painting of the original studio by Eduardo's eldest son, Pedro Chillida, hangs in the former family villa, now used for special events in the museum grounds.

Up the stairs, where a polished parquet floor warms the mezzanine, we are drawn into the more intimate spaces of the hayloft, a hush of wood sculptures and works on paper. From here, high above the oak, beech and magnolia trees, the vistas open out on to a green carpet from a small window that highlights the placement of sculptures within the 12-hectare (30-acre) park.

Built with its back flat to the wind and sheltered by plane trees, the Zabalaga Farmhouse is the public face of the Chillida legacy. Nestled into a wooded grove, up a steep rise, is the smaller, private villa once used by the family for gatherings and special events. Painter's canvas serves for curtains and upholstery, and walls are painted white in traditional gallery fashion. Old-fashioned panes and shutters make the villa feel like a conservatory, while paintings by other family members, including Pilar Belzunce, Chillida's widow, contribute a sense of immediacy, as if the house, now empty by design, has become yet another of the artist's interior spaces to explore.

The stunning canvas by Pedro Chillida emphasizes the idea of the farmhouse as studio, with its brooding, forge-like depths. The simple furniture cloaked in white and the polished wood floor encourage a sense of the sitting-room, too, as a space in which one might think about how place inspires art. For this place, the villa, park and farmhouse, now open to the world, inspired Eduardo Chillida, and here he brought together his art and life in a single, whole expression of his Basque roots.

OPPOSITE The clean white walls and furniture of the well-lit family villa serve as a neutral background for a collection of family paintings, including those by Chillida's widow, artist Pilar Belzunce.

RIGHT, TOP AND BOTTOM Chillida's dynamic play of steel on stone is a well-recognized mark of his work, as in his own favourite sculpture, *El Pieno del Viento*, or *The Comb of the Wind*, set at the base of San Sebastian's Mount Igeldo at the mouth of the harbour.

Catalan Collection
Village house, Perelada

Surrounded by vineyards and olive-groves producing some of Catalunya's finest 'liquid gold', the well-kept medieval village of Perelada sits in the flats of the agriculturally rich Alt Empordà region. The village, with its famous wine-producing *castillo*, casino and international music festival, boasts many well-restored façades mimicking faded stucco in a subtle range of authentic colours: ochre, ivory and pale yellows, bold statements of brick red, and that special Catalan blue that instantly conjures the thought of the nearby sea.

A ramble through the medieval streets leads to the Plaça Sant Domènec, shaded by the imposing structure of the historic *casa señorial*, Casa Avinyó. Here, a complicated arched entrance to the plaza shelters a street-front window displaying a seventeenth-century polychrome wooden angel, a nineteenth-century painting and a contemporary child's toy crèche. A hand-lettered sign proclaims, 'This is not a museum.' However, it is clear that it is something very special. Within iron-clad doors are more iron gates, more doors – an Ali Baba's cave of entrances that invites the visitor to browse through a huddle of seventeenth-century

OPPOSITE A gallery of religious and allegorical paintings welcomes visitors to the first-floor entrance door of the antiquarian's residence.

RIGHT, TOP A corner of the owner's bedroom displays favoured bronze sculptures before an early twentieth-century painting.

RIGHT, BOTTOM A gilt-framed Baroque marriage-bed, painted with a pair of sacred hearts, graces one of the guest rooms.

carved stone pilasters, oversized painted wooden frames and a gaily coloured miniature bus – a child's ride from a twentieth-century carousel.

Enric Serraplanas, elegant and courteous guardian and owner of this eclectic collection, greets us with the heavy brass bob dangling from his hand, the key to the ground-floor antiquarian gallery. We walk past a thousand treasures to a large, heavily settled Catalan door, originally painted oxblood red, with a small iron grille. The original key, hundreds of years old, hangs behind the door, proof of the unchanging quality of life in this *casa señorial* and in the village itself. It is behind these doors that the secrets of three hundred years of grandeur, neglect and careful restoration are revealed, in Serraplanas's private living-quarters.

Filtered light falls from a grand cupola perched three floors above the formal entrance courtyard. The blue-and-white plasterwork casts a softer glow on slate slabs that lie on their sides like much of Catalunya's village-street paving. A balcony opening, hidden behind a painting showing the life of some forgotten saint, confirms that this paved court was once an exterior passage from the plaza to the ancient monastery behind. With that perfect combination of thick, well-worn stone steps and graceful iron-work banister, the staircase ascends past a gallery of historical and contemporary paintings to approach the first-floor entrance to the main living-quarters.

LEFT, TOP In a simply furnished guest room, an original painted red table and blue doors wear their years gracefully and provide a colourful tribute to rustic Catalan furnishings.

LEFT, BOTTOM A single large oriental carpet links the elegant drawing-room and its furniture of different periods and styles.

From the landing, one can admire the restored glazed wooden gallery that connects a cluster of bedrooms to the common living-spaces. This entrance leads to the open foyer, which houses a museum-quality collection of Romanesque capitals. Wooden doors, painted, panelled and hung by original hardware, define the warren of interior spaces, one leading on to the next in a game of doors — doors to rooms, to armoires, to cupboards and to hidden spaces. Their surfaces richly textured and colourfully painted with the hues of earth and sky and sea, these Catalan doors, set off by deep-red hexagonal floor-tiles and handsome carpets, are still bright after three hundred years.

A pair of these doors opens invitingly on to a sitting-room, a combination of gallery and card-room. The lavish display of a lifetime's collection of paintings and sculptures delightfully distracts the eye from a pair of buttercup-yellow silk-brocade Empire-style chairs glowing in the morning sun. The house faces south, with the tall windows spilling light into the dark corners of the vaulted ceilings so typical of Catalan houses.

The master suite opens off the main sitting-room and serves as office and library; it is dominated by paintings from Serraplanas's modern collection. The alcove bed is a curious fantasy of four peacock posts set off by an eighteenth-century tapestry depicting an exotic forest in the same tones of blue that trim the door panels.

LEFT, TOP A collection of Catalan *dolls* (water-jugs) and rustic pottery parades around the traditionally tiled kitchen.

LEFT, BOTTOM A pair of blue-painted corner cupboards housing delicate ceramics echoes the colours of the elaborately painted doors in the dining-room.

OPPOSITE A modern Catalan dining-table and -chairs provide a focus for the room and its stunning collection of ceramic tiles, platters and spice dishes.

Sequestered away in a similar alcove in a guest room is a Baroque painted religious headboard from the inland region of Olot. The painted armoire doors, left in their original state, together with a few well-chosen wooden sculptures, reflect the near-monastic feeling of this capacious room, furnished as it is with a simple armchair and a Baroque red side-table.

Both kitchen and dining-room are whitewashed, with painted-wood cupboards that house yet further collections – of rustic Catalan pottery, antique regional porcelain and spice cellars. Typical corner-built cupboards are painted that graceful blue that haunts a summer sky, evoking a cool and quiet atmosphere around the dining-table and -chairs.

Although a treasury of fine art and historical pieces, Casa Avinyó holds its past lightly, the wealth of images and sculptures serving to divert the eye from a harsher world rather than weighing heavily on its owner's shoulders. Each piece, lovingly catalogued, signifies a memory, a souvenir or a personal event. That first warning sign, 'This is not a museum', comes to mind, and it is impossible to disagree. This is a very comfortable and gentle household, serving its owner with grace and beauty. Within the walls of the grand medieval home, Serraplanas has created a curiously dynamic collection of Spain's past with his discerning modern eye.

LEFT, TOP AND BOTTOM Displayed like independent sculptures, this important collection of Romanesque capitals provides a weighty balance to the colourful painted Catalan door.

OPPOSITE A campaign desk and painted chair serve as a bedroom office, while the peacock-post bed and commode tuck into the owner's sleeping-alcove.

Country Quietude
Bed and breakfast, Galicia

This little-known part of Spain is as green and wooded as more northern European regions, so for those accustomed to thinking of Spain as the bone-dry, red-roofed landscapes and villages of Andalucía, the Galician icons of green hydrangeas, silver-leafed eucalyptus and slate roofs will surprise and delight. Casa do Castelo de Andrade, a lovely rural guest house, lies hidden at the end of a long, narrow road high above the ragged coast of western Spain. Winding up through a dense eucalyptus forest, the woods give way to manicured fields and then a charming entrance of stone and slate, an emblem of the cool Galician landscape. Palms and kiwi, calla lilies and roses mix in the generous hedgerows that line the roads and fill the gardens of this beautifully restored traditional farmhouse.

Sharing its name with the nearby historic castle of Andrade, Casa do Castelo de Andrade was probably originally part of the extended castle property that served the lord of the manor as a house for his farmers, as well as acting, according to legend, as his rustic love-nest.

Galicia is a contrast in texture and colour, and the Casa do Castelo de Andrade emulates the regional spirit. Linen curtains edged with lace peek from behind thick double windows set into rust-coloured walls finished with bare stone. Ferns and hydrangeas soften the strong edges of the three-hundred-year-old house and outbuildings, flourishing in the cool Galician climate and the nearby warren of river *rías* – estuaries, with their

LEFT, TOP An iron-and-stone balcony projects off one of the guest suites in the main section of the house.

LEFT, BOTTOM Tinted stucco and painted blue trim create a warm welcome at the front door.

OPPOSITE As seen from the front door, the wood-and-stone granary wing houses guest bedrooms and the ground-floor library.

deltas, wetlands and wild beaches. A curtain of eucalyptus shelters the house from the sea, and the peaceful sound of water and birds prevails.

The charm of the coloured stucco and the stone walls finished with a signature blue trim draws guests into the cluster of low buildings, just two storeys high. 'This is a very old colour, this blue. On the windows, behind the green, behind the red, behind *all* the colours, is *this* blue', owner Alberto Morales explains. The pastel blue, like all woad paint, refers back to the early days, when the pigment residue left from dyers' vats was mixed with various media and used to paint the wooden trim on windows, doors and carts. This historic blue runs across Europe, from the sunny deep blues of France's Midi to the soft grey-blues of Scandinavia, and even jumps the North Sea to Scotland. Here in the Pontedueme region, the blue remains as one reminder, as much as the bagpipers and the language, that Galicia is the Celtic edge of Spain.

The bold use of colour is evident throughout the region, with startling bright tangerine and deep ultramarine washing over unadorned fishermen's houses. Here inside this *casa rural* the colours of the tinted plaster reflect a soft and gentle light and seem to filter the outside world. Ocean fog drifts up an open field to the house and across a 3-metre-wide (10 feet) window, which, in the sitting-area, frames the ever-altering view and reveals the passing light that changes from hour to hour. The curtain of haze gives way to sun later in the day. 'The window, this large window, is not a design. When I bought this place, it was an open door; it was just a rational decision to close it as a simple window,' Morales

OPPOSITE A well-lit sitting-area features original Galician farmhouse furniture.

RIGHT, TOP Large slate tiles pave the dining-area, with its long convivial table.

RIGHT, BOTTOM High-backed farmhouse settees overlook the changing light on fields and forests through a large picture window.

recalls. So this 'simple and rational' window holds the cosy interior lightly within.

Each room of the Casa do Castelo de Andrade is plainly furnished, using the same balanced approach, as Morales explains: 'I don't like everything rural. This is a mix of modern and old. Well, not so modern.' A darkened sitting-room and reception lead to the bright area where Morales offers coffee and thoughts. He searches to refine his ideas, as if the rooms should speak for themselves: 'Rustic is too heavy here, all this dark stone. This light is important. I like the big window and the white stone.'

The furniture is typical of farmhouses in Galicia. Long benches with high backs protect from draughts and cold. The original kitchen with its corner fireplace still serves the dining-area, where a charming old drop-leaf dining-table featuring a single leg complements a collection of furniture in a regional folk-art style. A tree trunk made into a cupboard, another forming a salt box, and a rustic beehive seem as modern as sculptures in this large and spacious room. The open dining-area is paved with soft-grey slate tiles, which flow from the entrance of the main house to a secluded walled garden at the back. Beeswax candles scent the house with honey.

A separate wing in the former granary houses a collection of charming bedrooms and a ground-floor library. Colour defines each of these rooms: the library is a soft, sand-coloured ochre; a blue bedroom recalls the sea; a pristine chamber is washed with white. The library itself needs no more decoration than a sheaf of wheat and a branch of eucalyptus on one side

LEFT, TOP AND BOTTOM A cream-coloured breakfast-service fills the wooden shelving and painted buffet next to a well-scrubbed kitchen table.

of the fireplace built into the corner. A clock stands still and unticking, as if time has been left on the doorstep. Flanking the blue entrance door, double windows become a wall of soft light moderated by passing clouds, a light that floods the reading-table and the book left enticingly open on it. The harmony of design creates an air of quiet as guests ebb and flow. Two comfortable wing chairs invite a closer look at a lovely little book of Galician poetry and prints near the fireplace, while a raffia basket and logs, a sturdy table and rush-seat farm chairs, complete the picture.

In the restful bedrooms, walls and ceilings harmonize with hand-painted bedside tables and headboards. Exposed beams and waxed wooden floors set off the pleasing arrangement of the simple furnishings – a rocking chair, hand-woven linen curtains, and those 'click-clack' ceramic switches and woven-cord electrical fittings, as pleasing to the eye as they are nostalgic, which all recall another era. Each room offers a private haven of repose enhanced by such thoughtful touches.

Back in the main building, the farmhouse kitchen is the calm centre of the house, painted and tiled in thick cream, its colour resembling that of the real cream served here with dark drinking chocolate and home-made biscuits. A large buffet holds enough dishes and glassware for a crowd, and breakfast crockery is on display – as much a sign of hospitality as an invitation to tea at the well-scrubbed table. From the kitchen, which offers the first view of visitors walking up the slate path to the door, Alberto Morales sets a refined and charming stage from which to enjoy Galicia and its very different sort of Spanish charm.

RIGHT, TOP A pristine, whitewashed bedroom is warmed by the soft textures of woven throws.

RIGHT, BOTTOM On cool Galician days, the library's simple stucco-faced fireplace creates a glowing focus.

OPPOSITE Delicate tones of rose pigment colour the walls and complement the pale-grey furniture of a favourite guest bedroom.

Urban Artistry

Apartment, Madrid

On entering the classic Madrileño apartment of designer Borja Azcarate, one discovers a fertile and exciting world, the elements of which are stitched together with innovative lighting. Azcarate welcomes clients and guests to his place by demonstrating the way in which carefully chosen and well-loved objects create a home as well as telling the tale of the personalities behind the scenes.

Despite being situated in a densely populated residential area, Azcarate's apartment lifts the spirits through a special blend of tranquillity and energy. The front part of the flat is a tightly clustered labyrinth of individual rooms opening one on to the other, with enticing inward-facing views. What looks to be at first a wall mirror is, in fact, an oversized, custom-built bull's-eye window, breaking the solid wall between the dining-room and the central sitting-room. Lit by Azcarate's signature industrial metal lamp, this generous circle of glass allows light, as well as a view, into the next room, creating the sense of watching an ever-changing painting. Azcarate, a devoted collector of the work of contemporary artist Charles Sandison, often projects Sandison's word-sculptures through this interior window and into the sitting-rooms next door. A pair of charcoal giants — wall-height figures that reach from floor to ceiling — when seen through the looking-glass window, heightens the play of scale in the dining-room and adjacent sitting-rooms. The formal monotone elements can be easily rearranged to suit Azcarate's needs, enabling him to use the rooms as galleries, reception areas or dining-spaces.

One of three intimate sitting-areas in the Madrid apartment of interior designer Borja Azcarate. A custom-made interior window offers a view of the adjacent dining-area and serves as a secondary source of natural light.

In the first of three sitting-areas, contemporary fabric covers the classic chairs, while Azcarate's twin loves of found objects and foundry-work merge in a low, iron-legged table. This signature piece supports a painted-glass mirror, becoming in itself a horizontal artwork.

Azcarate's love and appreciation of the arts was instilled in him through two family businesses — fine antiques and a leather-crafting factory — yet it is the clever and subtle lighting of his favourite objects and the rooms themselves that reveals his own finely tuned hand. Two fencing masks, poised at the entrance, are lit from a simple metal box resting on the floor, and thus become transformed into curious wall sconces; what seems a simple shelving unit propped in a corner is actually an ambient light sculpture; a stunning photographic work, printed on a transparent panel, is backlit and, illuminating the way to the bedroom and bathroom, draws one down a long, dark hall.

Azcarate's single bedroom is a soft haven of warm grey and rose. A charming painted panel from a theatrical backdrop becomes a suspended ceiling, and the French-style bed is guarded by a painted Indonesian doorframe and another working bull's-eye window. Framed and hung like a wall sculpture, the rescued Parisian window, complete with roof flashing,

PAGE 248 A detailed wooden model of a cathedral cupola stands at the entrance to a reception area for Azcarate's visiting clients. On the rear wall hangs an antique Chinese cartwheel, which has been hand-finished with layers of translucent paint over squares of vellum-like material.

PAGE 249 An antique ebony chest perched on a table lends gravitas to the small salon furnished with a collection of personal objects displayed on one of Azcarate's signature metal tables.

RIGHT The compact dining-room acts as an extension of the office and gallery, providing a place from which Azcarate projects ephemeral transparencies of artworks into the adjacent salons.

whimsically echoes a nearby collection of zinc building ephemera, a testament to the designer's passion for collecting.

'I love working with collectors', confesses Azcarate. 'They show their affections easily with what they buy.' He encourages his clients to invest their homes with their personal objects – just as he does, for example, by combining a well-used galvanized washing-tub, a wooden Chinese cartwheel and a driftwood mirror and elevating them to the status of a unified collection, displayed before a textured wall of vellum-like squares painted smoky charcoal-grey. Azcarate's love of the handcrafted is evident in solitary pieces, such as the fish-eye mirror originally created for a Mexico City restaurant and now hung in the spare and functional kitchen.

The underlying neutral grey colour resurfaces in the dark-coal parquet found throughout the apartment, a strong backdrop to Azcarate's many theatrical pieces. Inspired by the historic white-and-black interiors of early rural Spanish houses, with their white walls and black-painted mourning furniture, Azcarate breathes new life into the ideal of Spanish style. Reaching back to this austere history, with its echo of monastic neutrality, he defines his own design rules with a contemporary edge, yet grounds his style rationally in the restrained past, and plays a delicate game of visual and intellectual contrasts that springs from a well-educated choice of furnishings, light and space.

RIGHT, TOP A dedicated collector, Azcarate displays zinc and lead architectural details on a shelf in his bedroom.

RIGHT, BOTTOM Another zinc detail – this one of the Greek god Hermes, from an exterior frieze – serves as an unusual shade for a standing lamp.

OPPOSITE Azcarate's signature iron-framed, mirror-topped low table is one of the many sculptural pieces to be found in this dynamic sitting-area, which features such diverse materials as resin, wood and leather.

Grand Style
Luxury hotel, Sanlúcar La Mayor

Like a strong regional accent announcing that you have arrived in the South, nothing shouts 'Andalucía!' more than the colours that designer Manuel Gavira uses inside and out at this renewed urban resort. With relaxed refinement, the historic Hacienda Benazuza elBullihotel welcomes guests with the passionate embrace of Spain's southernmost region.

Away from the flurry of Seville, the Hacienda Benazuza dominates a quiet neighbourhood in the small provincial town of Sanlúcar La Mayor. This updated tenth-century hacienda is also home to the two-Michelin-starred La Alqueria, the second restaurant of renowned chef Ferran Adrià, whose three-star El Bulli north of Barcelona has the reputation as one of the best restaurants in the world.

The notable Hacienda Benazuza, like much of the Seville area, fell under the spell of the 1992 World's Fair and was converted to a luxury hotel. Now a breath of fresh Andalucían air has blown the last cobwebs away and revealed the grand structure and dimensions of the original Moorish fortified estate. Sevillano designer Manuel Gavira, whose studio/showroom is sited near the yellow sand of the Plaza de Toros in Seville, undertook the restoration of the grand historic estate. With a controlled hand and an eye for detail, Gavira aims to remind us, at every turn of a corridor or entry into a courtyard, that we are, above all, in Andalucía. A stroll through the original gardens is defined by a tiled line of cyan blue running from pool to fountain to Moorish canal, a focus for the eye just as the trickle of water attracts the ear during the evening

OPPOSITE Fragrant Seville orange-trees and graceful palms herald the formal entrance into the pristine white luxury of the Hacienda Benazuza.

OVERLEAF Moorish features adorn the tenth-century courtyards as white plays off strong colour to define the architectural details of the many inner enclosures.

promenade. Where Seville is the noisy corrida, bars and chic strolls through the city's orange-blossom-scented streets, this rural hacienda is an oasis of calm and good design.

Gavira began with the imposing walled structure that served as fort, retreat and village for more than a thousand years. With a broad sweep of traditional colours, he painted over the tenth-century bones of the white-plastered hacienda with a brighter and more modern palette, linking the interior spaces – courtyards, patios and shaded walks – with the oxblood-red, polished terracotta tiles. Chief among these central courtyards is the Palm Court, frescoed a shady, muted red and anchored by four towering palms forming a leaf-fringed canopy. Graceful arcades enclose this convivial square, and shelter paintings, sideboards, seating and the entrance to the salon, bar and a casual café. A solitary bull's head, hung on one wall, gives a silent nod to the nineteenth-century life of the ranch, where breeder Pablo Romero once produced some of the finest fighting bulls in Andalucía.

The many courtyards hint at the past life of the hacienda, which was as much a fortified village as a single estate. The spaces are large and graceful, cloistered or open by turn, but above all coloured with the bright pigments of *alvaro*, *anil* and *amalgara* – the classic palette of yellow, blue and red that is used throughout for the traditional estate buildings. Thick stone walls defend the interiors from the heat, while a cool timber overhang, underpainted in blue and green, echoes the blue-and-white plasterwork. The 'La Higuera' patio shelters an ancient horse-watering trough that now serves as a contemporary fountain in the courtyard, where a solitary fig tree reaches up to the sun. Discreet staff, dressed in

OPPOSITE A gold-leafed Baroque bed dressed with immaculate linens dominates one of the hotel's favoured suites.

RIGHT, TOP AND BOTTOM Bronze fixtures and authentic Moorish tiles embellish one of the hotel's luxurious bathrooms.

formal black-and-white linen, move quietly through this colourful backdrop, delivering an afternoon aperitif of *fino y jamón* on fine La Cartuja black-and-white plates. Further play with colour is evident in the bouquets of flowers as colourful and fluted as a flamenco dancer's dress, and in a leafy bougainvillea that flirts in a breeze alongside an iron gate as its two filigree shadows are thrown against an ochre wall.

It is by means of this judicious use of strong pigment that the true colour of Andalucía is revealed: white – bleached-bone white, lime-wash white, waxy blossom white. Capped with a ruffle of Andalucían roof tiles, flat white walls, their edges softened by centuries of plaster whitewash, connect a seventeenth-century chapel tower to the main Moorish entrance. The clean white of the fortress's arched tower is echoed everywhere, from the limed trunks of fragrant orange-trees to a holy-water font filled with pearly orange-blossoms. White reappears in a graceful marble column supporting a shaded arch, and a perfectly ironed linen bedsheet. This play of white against colour, whether the deep blue of the southern sky or the yellow-ochre of the sand, defines the clean edges of the massive exteriors. It is only once one passes through heavy wooden doors that the flat, wide walls give way to a Baroque exuberance of fabric and furnishing within the interior.

While life outside the hacienda might be as rugged as the vast southern landscapes, inside Benazuza, grace and civility prevail. Broad passages rather like elongated living-rooms connect the forty-four guest rooms. These colourful carpeted hallways, furnished with deep-seated English-style velour chairs and polished wooden tables, are tempered by the shuttered windows, offering a respite from the exterior. Capacious

LEFT, TOP AND BOTTOM Weaving formal lawn and native cacti together, water plays a running game of fountains, pools and canals throughout the extensive gardens that surround the hacienda.

OPPOSITE A delicate dance of water into a square pool cools the dappled courtyard garden, as well as creating soft background music.

bedrooms reflect a studied luxury that includes gold-leafed and painted headboards, frescoed ceilings, and plastered fireplaces textured with interesting details; gold-thread passementerie on a table; a polished silver *pebetero*, or incense-burner; and an ironwork convent grille peeking into a bathroom. Such details recall the Baroque influence that marks a transition from ornate Moorish design to eighteenth-century wealth.

Were Spain able to be defined by one element, it might be the abundant ironwork that frets the door and window balconies of so many residences and buildings. Even here, in the simplest narrow handrail, or long stair-rail decorated with a garland of boxwood, it plays a role as a defining material. Neither heavy nor too ornate, this simple ironwork balances elaborate basketry as these two opposing elements — one permanent, the other ephemeral — weave through the many courtyards.

As distinctive as the iron balconies and gates, these woven works texture the walls and corners of the hacienda. Large natural-fibre filters, once used for the olive-press, now serve as doormats; thick rush awnings drape from shuttered windows to shade rooms from the hot southern sun; woven wainscoting and baskets filled with chickpeas define a casual dining-room. In the large Palm Court, ferns and palm fronds echo the handmade basketry found throughout the estate and soften the sense of the sturdy fortress's more militant past.

In the latest incarnation of hacienda living, Manuel Gavira has given the Hacienda Benazuza a new life of grand luxury, stemming from a grander history and celebrating the ancient spirit of al-Andalus. The element of long tradition gives texture to the solid framework, while a firm sense of modern purpose freshens and lends new energy to a thousand years of hacienda style.

LEFT, TOP AND BOTTOM Delicate ironwork gates are used to divide arcaded spaces, while a souvenir of early hacienda transport stands fast.

OPPOSITE Early romantic graffiti on the eighteenth-century chapel, a favoured wedding site for contemporary Sevillianos.

Style Directory

Hotels

Can Bonastre Wine Resort (pp. 38–45)
The wine resort is located thirty-five minutes from Barcelona, at the foot of the Montserrat mountains.

Crta. B-224 Km. 13,2
08733 Masquefa (BCN)
Tel. (Hotel): +34 93 772 87 67
Tel. (Wine resort): +34 93 772 61 6
Website: canbonastre.com

Casa do Castelo Andrade (pp. 238–45)
Owner Alberto Morales manages this quiet country hotel in Galicia.

Lugar do Castelo de Andrade,
s/n. 15.608-PONTEDEUME-A Coruña
Tel.: +34 981 43 38 39
Fax: +34 981 43 34 66
Website: casteloandrade.com

Casa Grande Fontao (pp. 178–91)
Owner Mari Freire welcomes guests to her family home and private hotel.

Lugar de Fontao 1A
15639 Miño, La Coruña, Galicia, España
Tel: +34 981 782 772
Fax: +34 981 782 717
Website: casagrandefontao.com

Cortijo El Esparragal (pp. 22–31)
This is both a working ranch and a charming hotel near Seville.

Carretera Sevilla
41860 Gerena, Spain
Tel: +34 955 782 702
Website: elesparragal.com

Hacienda Benazuza elBullihotel (pp. 254–69)
Ferran Adria offers his famous cuisine in a luxury hotel setting near Seville.

41800 Sanlúcar La Mayor
Seville
Tel: +34 955 703 344
Fax: +34 955 703 410
Website: elbullihotel.com

Hotel Itureggi (pp. 134–45)
This quiet country retreat overlooks the sea near Getaria.

Barrio Azkizu
20808 Getaria (Guipúzcoa)
Tel: +34 943 896 134
Website: hoteliturregi.com

Marqués de Riscal 'City of Wine' (pp. 164–77)
'Ciudad del Vino', located in Elciego (Alava), is a complex comprising the oldest winery of Rioja, the winery of Marqués de Riscal (1858), and a new building designed by the Canadian architect Frank O. Gehry.

Calle Torrea, 1
01340 Elciego (Alava)
Tel: +34 945 60 60 00
Fax: +34 945 60 60 23
E-mail: marquesderiscal@marquesderiscal.com
Website: marquesderiscal.com

Parador Hostal dos Reis Católicos (pp. 120–33)
This historic hotel is located on the main square, next to the famous Cathedral of Santiago de Compostela.

Praza Obradoiro 1
15705 Santiago De Compostela
Tel. +34 981 582 200
Website: parador.es

The Pavilions of Les Cols (pp. 156–63)
Owner/Chef Fina Puigdevall provides stellar accommodation to match her avant-garde cuisine.

Mas les Cols
Carretera de la Canya
17800 OLOT (Girona)
Tel.: +34 972 26 92 09
Fax: +34 972 27 07 27
E-mail: lescols@lescols.com
Website: lescols.com

Designers

Baruc Corazón (pp. 46–57)
Corazón designs and redefines the classic button-down shirt at his Madrid boutique.

Calle Piamonte, 19
28004 Madrid, ESPAÑA
Tel.: +34 91 310 25 59
E-mail: info@baruccorazon.com
Website: baruccorazon.com

Borja Azcarate (pp. 98–107, 246–53)
Borja Azcarate Interiores S.L
Paseo de Eduardo Dato 8,
Madrid 28001
Tel: +34 91 319 11 30

Manuel Gavira (pp. 254–69)
Gracia Fernandez Palacios, 3
41001 Seville
Tel: + 34 954 22 67 03
E-mail: interior@manuelgavira.com

Manuel Morales De Jódar (pp. 192–203)
Morales is also an antiques dealer.

C/Trajano, 52
41002 Seville
Tel: +34 629704499

Javier Muñoz (pp. 164–77)
Calle Velazquez, 158
Madrid 28002
Tel: +34 915 642 463
Fax: +34 915 633 342
E-mail: javier-munoz@javier-munoz.com
Website: javiermunoz.es

Daniel Rotaeche Designs (pp. 134–45)
Fuenterrabía, 31
20005 San Sebastián
Tel: +34 943 471 412

Gaspar Sobrino (pp. 32–37)
Les Charmelites
Madrid
Tel: +34 600 037 249
E-mail: info@lescharmelites.es

Thomas Urquijo (pp. 72–83)
Ronda de Atocha, 37
28012 Madrid
Tel: +34 91 506 2972

Architects

Pablo Carvajal – architect (pp. 72–83)
Rafael Calvo, 42
Madrid 28010
Website: pablocarvajal.com

Frank O. Gehry (pp. 164–77)
Gehry Partners, LLP
12541 Beatrice Street
Los Angeles, CA 90066
United States of America
Tel: +1 310 482 3000
Fax: +1 310 482 3006
Website: foga.com

Joaquin Montero (pp. 214–25)
Garibai 3–4° Derecha,
20004 Donostia-San Sebastián (Gipuzkoa)
Website: joaquinmontero.com

RCR Arquitectes (pp. 156–63)
Passeig de Blay 34, 2n
17800, Olot (Girona, Catalunya)
Website: rcrarquitectes.es

Antiques Dealers

Miguel Caiceo (pp. 146–55)
Basero 11
28005 Madrid, Spain

Serge Castella (pp. 108–119)
Masos de Calabuig
17483 Bascara, Spain
Tel.: +34 972 551 664;
+34 653 622 620

Enric Serraplanas (pp. 226–37)
Plaça Sant Domènec 5
17491 Peralada, Spain
Tel.: +34 972 538 082

Art Galleries

Miquel Alzueta (pp. 84–97)
Tel: +34 93 238 97 50
E-mail: info@galeriamiquelalzueta.com
Website: galeriamiquelalzueta.com

Museu Chillida-Leku (pp. 214–25)
Bº Jauregui, 66
E-20120 Hernani (Gipuzkoa)
Tel.: +34 943 336006
Website: eduardo-chillida.com

Moisés Tibau (pp. 204–13)
Gallery showroom in Cadaqués located behind
Casa Blaua (pp. 58–71).
Ac N0 20-
17488 GE Cadaqués
E-mail: fullblast@adslmail.es
Website: moisestibau.com

Spanish Tourist Office: Website: spain.info

First published 2009 by

Merrell Publishers Limited
81 Southwark Street
London SE1 0HX

merrellpublishers.com

British Library Cataloguing-in-Publication Data:
Hill, Kate
Spanish style
1. Interior decoration – Spain
I. Title II. Clinch, Tim
747'.0946

ISBN 978-1-8589-4458-6

Produced by Merrell Publishers Limited
Designed by Martin Lovelock
Copy-edited by Kirsty Seymour-Ure
Proof-read by Elizabeth Tatham

Printed and bound in China